THE END OF TRAINING

How Business Simulations Are Reshaping Business Training

by Michael S. Vaughan
With Kate Skarsten and Stephen Kirkpatrick

REGIS
LEARNING
SOLUTIONS

Regis Learning Solutions
Golden, CO

Published by

Keystone Business Press

keystonebusinesspress.com

A division of

REGIS
LEARNING
SOLUTIONS

www.regislearning.com
433 Park Point Drive, Suite 225
Golden, CO 80401
(303) 526-3005

Printed in the United States of America

Contents

PREFACE

My fundamental belief is that most corporate training is ineffective.

I don't make this statement lightly. I've been part of the training industry for nearly fifteen years. I have authored and delivered hundreds of workshops, measurement tools, e-learning modules, and everything in between. From intense small group training to huge enterprise-level e-learning, I've done it all.

Like most people in the industry, I was excited about the advent of e-learning. I thought we finally had a way to engage large numbers of employees with effective, motivational training. After a while, however, I realized that e-learning wasn't all it was cracked up to be. Despite my different designs and approaches, the e-learning modules I designed and released weren't helping anything. Employees clicked through the training, but their behavior didn't really change. The same thing was true of most workshops. As a facilitator, I remember receiving nothing but smiles on evaluations, then watching people hurry back to their work demands and thinking to myself–they won't change.

In 2003, I joined forces with two other adult learning experts to create Regis Learning Solutions, a company committed to training that makes a difference. As we began to formulate a new vision, we asked the tough questions: Why does training in corporate America ignore what learning professionals know to be true about adult learning principles? Why do we, as an industry, still churn out the same tired, lecture-based training, "death by PowerPoint" presentations, and "click-through" e-learning programs when we know that people don't learn that way? Why have we accepted boring, ineffective training for so many years? Why hasn't anyone been able to design training that really works?

The problem certainly isn't a shortage of options. Today more than ever, we are overloaded with the amount of training and information available, from massive e-learning catalogues to seminars in hotel ballrooms; from mom-and-pop training providers to multi-million-dollar consulting firms. In addition to the training, there are volumes of research, hundreds of business degree programs, and millions of workshops available to corporations. Yet employees still suffer from a gap between knowing what to do and actually being able to do it.

As we studied the situation, the leadership team at RLS found gaps between:

- The way employees are trained and the way adults learn best
- Corporate strategies and training strategies
- How much people know and how little they can actually do
- The delivery/types of training available and the need to improve employee performance quickly
- The focus of many off-the-shelf training catalogues and the need to change employee perception

Addressing these gaps became the major focus of our company. After years of research, experience, and some trial and error, we became convinced that business simulations best answer our concerns.

For too long, businesses have been slow to adopt simulations, due in part to expense and the unique design challenges, as well as an overall lack of familiarity with the genre. The evolution of technology and its capacity to make more powerful and easily customizable simulations available to the business world at lower price points than ever before have changed all of that, however. More companies now use simulations, and more simulation vendors are coming to market. Business simulations are increasingly advanced, with new innovations emerging almost daily. These are exciting times for simulations, and I am energized by the fact that a genre I have worked with and nurtured for that last twenty years is finally getting the recognition it so richly deserves.

About a year ago, a monthly trade magazine ran a cover story on simulations, proclaiming them to be the next generation of e-learning. Mass adoption of simulations in the business environment, the author argued, was just around the corner.

It may surprise you to know that I was conflicted by the article. On one hand, I was thrilled to see simulations get the attention I knew they deserved.

On the other hand, I was dismayed by the hype that the article built. I had seen the trend to simulations coming for some time, but the media and industry attention suddenly seemed to reach a fever pitch— with simulation-related books, articles, vendor-sponsored "webinars" cropping up almost by the minute. The evidence, in short, was all around us. Simulations finally were gathering steam and generating buzz— or whatever that X factor is called that ultimately propels a new discipline from the outskirts of an industry to its center stage.

At the same time, I could see training professionals becoming both frustrated with and sophisticated about learning technologies. Today's buyers lived through the dot-com boom—and subsequent bust—and clearly remember the euphoria of the '90s, when e-learning was heralded as a panacea for all of the industry's ills. Today's buyers, well-versed in the delivery of workshops and the shortcomings of e-learning's, have been there and done that and are no longer blind idealists. They are more critical (and rightly so) of the abilities of simulations or any training tool, and their role in enhancing performance. They fully realize that while simulation solutions bring many benefits, there is no true panacea for training and performance-related issues in the workplace.

Experiential solutions like simulations are reshaping business training. We are coming to the end of the training solution as a band-aid and entering a new era of training department as strategic partner. This book is meant to serve as a resource and guide for helping you navigate through the hype and selectively integrate simulations into your business.

Michael S. Vaughan

ACKNOWLEDGEMENTS

This book would not have been possible without the support of everyone at Regis Learning Solutions. We would especially like to thank our CEO Peggy Steele, a leader in the field of simulations, who provided invaluable guidance and encouragement.

Kevin Himmel, senior instructional designer and lead performance consultant, helped us connect the design and business aspects of simulations. He also provided patient feedback and direction as we created the SIMTEC model.

Patrick Kelling, who wrote, fact checked, and researched tirelessly. We could not have written this book without him.

Beth Jusino, editor extraordinaire, took all of the pieces we wrote and turned them into a book.

Rod Walker, who showed us that a business model can be beautiful and that a simulation really can reflect the real world.

Last but certainly not least, Sarah Bohle, whose article in *Training* magazine provided our original inspiration, graciously worked with us to refine our vision and focus our efforts.

INTRODUCTION

If workplace simulations were movie stars, their publicist would deserve a raise. In the last two years, simulations have been discussed in countless newspaper articles and conference sessions. They have been featured on the covers of several leading magazines. They even have been the topic of numerous CNN business segments.

Yet, the question lingers: Is all the hype surrounding simulations, well, just that?

Not according to Gartner Inc. The Stamford, CT research firm recently predicted that computerized simulations will become a critical component of approximately seventy percent of all e-learning courseware by 2006.

Why are so many of today's organizations rushing to implement simulations? With business changing at breakneck speed and a leadership gap looming on the horizon, CLOs and other business leaders are scrambling to find ways to provide workers with the critical skills they need for the next generation of business.

Faced with these challenges, it's no wonder that so many companies are turning to simulations. By immersing learners in environments that mimic the complexities of the real-world workplace and challenging them to take risks and make mistakes without real-world risk, simulations not only possess the ability to decrease the time it takes for workers to learn new skills, they also possess incredible potential to create rich, engaging learning experiences that can't be matched by conventional learning interventions.

Amidst all of the excitement, however, learning professionals face a harsh reality. New simulation vendors are coming to market daily. Technology is advancing at an unprecedented pace. And while simulations have been used in the workplace for decades in association with strategic modeling activities, their use as a learning tool within corporate environments is a relatively new phenomenon. As a result, quantitative research and benchmarks for successfully leveraging simulations often are hard for learning professionals to come by—making the simulation landscape confusing even for the most seasoned training practitioners.

The purpose of this book is to help you sort through the confusion surrounding workplace simulations and to answer the myriad questions that so many learning professionals have about them—from what they are and what they are capable of accomplishing to best practices and how-tos for successfully leveraging them within your organization.

This book is intended for anyone who is interested in harnessing the power of simulations to transform learning experiences and accelerate speed to performance, including:

- Training directors
- Training managers
- Chief learning officers and other learning executives
- Human resources specialists
- Executive-level decision makers
- Managers, business-unit leaders, and others interested in creating dynamic learning experiences that drive performance and create competitive advantage

What You'll Learn

- What workplace simulations are and the different types of workplace simulations that exist today.
- How to determine whether your business is ready for simulations—and, if not, how to employ practical, proven tips for getting your organization ready to harness the power of simulations.
- Questions to ask yourself when deciding whether simulations (or other types of learning interventions) are right for a given need.

11

- How to select the right simulation for the right need.
- How to ensure that the simulation you select lives up to its potential and delivers the results your organization requires.
- How to balance the risk/reward equation so that the results your simulation delivers justify the time and money your organization invests in its creation and deployment.
- How to navigate the process of implementing a simulation successfully from start to finish–from selecting a simulation, achieving buy-in, and marketing to effective facilitation, follow-up, and measurement.

What's the Payoff?

By the end of this book, we hope that you and your organization will achieve the following outcomes:

- Deliver rich, interactive training that closely approximates the real-world work environment.
- Accelerate speed to performance (decreasing the time it takes for workers to learn new skills), allowing workers to learn in days or weeks what would traditionally take them months of on-the-job or traditional training.
- Afford learners ample opportunity for hands-on practice and the freedom to make and learn from their mistakes–without real-life risk to your business.
- Enhance learning retention and transfer of learning to the job compared to other forms of instruction.
- Teach learners to apply multiple workplace skills simultaneously in ways that help them understand the vital interplay of various skill sets in the workplace.
- Change learners' mindsets from linear, cause-and-effect thinking to systemic thinking about the intended and unintended consequences of their

actions–both to their own department and to the organization as a whole.

- Generate substantial return on investment (ROI) for your organization through the appropriate use of simulations.

What's Included?

This book is divided into three sections:

Part One–Why the Hype?–examines the current excitement surrounding simulations and the evidence supporting their ability to transform workplace learning. Part One also examines the history of simulations and the drivers contributing to their recent popularity among businesses.

Part Two–Understanding Business Simulations–provides a detailed understanding of what simulations are, as well as information regarding the various types of simulations that exist today. This section answers critical questions such as "What makes a simulation a simulation?" and "What's behind the various types of simulation designs?" Part II introduces the SIMTEC model to explain the key components of a simulation.

Part Two also explores the criteria for choosing to use a simulation. In this section, you'll find helpful diagnostic questions to ask yourself as you navigate the process of determining whether a simulation is right for a given business need. The Learning Solution Decision Tree walks you through this process.

Finally, Part Two uses case studies to examine simulations in action. Two different cases are used to illuminate each aspect of the SIMTEC model and explain how simulations work in the real world.

Part Three–What Really Makes Simulations Work?–introduces best practices that have helped other organizations successfully introduce simulations. The practices covered in Part Three will help you navigate the step-by-step process of implementing a workplace simulation from start to finish—from selecting and working with a vendor and selling your simulation to key stakeholders to internal marketing, testing and implementation, delivery, follow-up, measurement and reporting of results, and beyond.

Finally, the **Epilogue** provides a sneak peek of the future of simulation training and examines the numerous advancements that experts anticipate will revolutionize simulations–and workplace learning–in years to come.

①

Part One:

WHY THE HYPE?

Gartner estimates that about seventy percent of e-learning will be replaced by simulations by 2007. Brandon Hall Research Inc. estimates that simulations will grow to a $6.1 billion market by 2006 and by 2011 will be worth $37 billion.[1] Meanwhile, new simulations designs and technologies are being released daily. Are simulations merely another flavor of the month, or are they here to stay? More importantly, how do you know what to look for when buying or building a simulation?

The U.S. Air Force had a problem: they knew that most of their combat losses occurred during a pilot's first ten missions. After that, deaths dropped dramatically. If the Air Force could get pilots through those first encounters safely, they knew they would dramatically reduce combat losses. But how could new pilots get the experience they needed to survive without getting killed in the process?

Major Richard Moody Suter had an answer. He advocated the creation of the Red Flag training simulation, an environment so realistic that a new pilot could "fly" his first ten combat missions in a controlled setting. The pilot could get the experience he needed to survive without the mortal risk. Suter hoped that when a new pilot went into actual combat after going through Red Flag, he would already have "survived" his most vulnerable period.

Today, the Air Force is using the Red Flag simulation with great success. "Realistic training initiatives completely transformed the culture of Air Force training," wrote Maj. Alexander Berger in USAF's *Air & Space Power Journal*. "With the advent of Red Flag, [the train-the-way-you-fight mentality] became firmly entrenched in the vernacular of aircrews everywhere."[2]

Pilots entering Red Flag tend to arrive planning to demonstrate how great they are *individually*. They have something to prove. As they go through the simulation, though, they begin to understand that their individual success depends on the entire team. Ground crews, fire crews, rescue teams, and mission control must all work in harmony in order for the pilots to stay alive during combat.

During the first few rounds of Red Flag, pilots receive reports of their individual performance. By the end of the simulation, pilots no longer are shown their personal results. Instead, they see a report for the entire team. This shift from individual to group results underscores the critical nature of teamwork during a mission. It also emphasizes the importance of "training" experiences that effectively change behavior to align with strategic goals.

Red Flag does more than encourage teamwork; it saves lives.

Behind the Hype

Today, the business world faces many of the same issues—though on a different scale—that led the Air Force to create Red Flag. Employees encounter steep learning curves during their first year on the job and are less effective than they are likely to be later in their careers. Employers face a retention problem when frustrated new staff members leave jobs at a higher rate than those who have mastered a position over a number of years.

Business simulations offer an innovative new way to answer this challenge. If you have worked in the training industry for any significant period of time, you may have noticed that the hype surrounding simulations today sounds suspiciously similar to the promises made about previous "flavor of the month" training trends. E-learning, blended learning, computer-based training (CBT), and a host of other methodologies all were supposed to "revolutionize" training and change the way employees learn. Few, if any, lived up to the promises made.

Nearly every training industry professional has tried "the latest thing" to meet her training needs, sometimes with great success. Certainly, each popular method affected workplace training and did indeed change the industry to an extent, but none lived up to their full promise or potential. Not one was the Holy Grail that magazines and training pundits promised.

Simulations are reshaping today's business training

According to a 2004 Accenture study that examined high-performance workforce issues, seventy-seven percent of executives across all industries are dissatisfied with the progress their training departments are making to align learning strategies with business goals.

One of the reasons for this disconnect is that too many business leaders view training as a temporary fix instead of a long-term strategic solution. Training departments disperse

17

their solutions as strategically as the office manager does offices supplies. Businesses see training as a tool like a pencil—important when you need it, but almost entirely unrelated to the business' goals or strategies.

Instead of integrating training budgets with the business strategy, companies often use them to fill a gap or react to an emergency. An employee might take a quick e-learning seminar to learn to read a financial statement, but the program is not likely to help her understand the purpose of financial statements, or how her new skill relates to the company's strategy. "Off-the-shelf" training programs may contain some references to company missions and values, but they don't effectively go beyond surface compliance to a real connection with strategic goals.

This disparity between learning experiences and strategic execution is not only common, it's also counterproductive.

At Regis Learning Solutions (RLS), we call this the *trainer triage mentality*. Trainers address problems that arise with the quickest, cheapest, and easiest solution that will solve the immediate problem, but without a focus on long-term impact. Unfortunately, the triage approach is only good for quick fixes—slap a Band-Aid on it and be done.

Over the last few years, the trainer triage approach has become easier and more tempting than ever. E-learning vendors have created enormous catalogues of on-line courses that equip trainers to react quickly and with very little effort to problems.

This is not necessarily a bad thing; e-learning courses offer solid, temporary fixes, but they should not be viewed as the end of training."

Fortunately, the era of trainer triage and catalog courses is coming to an end. In their place, businesses are focusing on innovative new programs that are directly tied to strategic goals and use experiential learning solutions. One of the most innovative solutions in this area is the business simulation.

The purpose of a business simulation is to reduce the time it takes learners to gain a deeper understanding of a business or to acquire new knowledge and skills that will help them effectively execute and evaluate business strategies. At RLS, we coined the term Speed to Performance™ to describe this process of acquiring new knowledge, skills, or attitudes.

Think about it this way: Your business is unique, with many processes, business units, products and services, strategies, goals, issues, and daily challenges. On top of all that, competition continually forces your company to change and improve. In your need to be quicker and better than your competitors, you seek the fastest training solutions available.

However, to truly improve performance in the long term, behavior needs to change. To change behavior, people require practice, which they usually obtain through experience. Quick training programs give your employees the foundational knowledge they need to understand what has to be done, but they will still lack the experience necessary to effectively execute and evaluate their actions. Gaining experience takes time and money, luxuries your business may not have. Thus, your mission is to shorten the time it takes for your employees to gain experience.

The knowing-doing gap

Amazon.com lists 17,994 business books published in 2004 alone. Millions of business-related courses are delivered annually. More and more people graduate with MBAs each year. Why then, with this wealth of knowledge that employees consume, do most businesses fall short of their goals?

In their book *The Knowing-Doing Gap: How Smart Companies Turn Knowledge into Action,* Jeffrey Pfeffer and Robert I. Sutton call this paradox the Knowing-Doing Gap. Most people know more than they actually can do. In the United States, for example, we know far more about healthy eating and exercising than we put into practice.

The authors relate that many organizations provide forty or more hours of training per year for each employee, yet few corporate goals are achieved. Accomplishments are often the result of a heroic effort from twenty percent of the employees, while the other eighty percent fail to apply their knowledge and skills toward executing strategy.[3] Why is there such a huge gap?

Pfeiffer and Sutton conclude that fears, beliefs, and lack of structure contribute to the problem. Experience fills the knowledge and comprehension gaps, and eventually builds confidence. Employees need to gain experience in an environment that will allow them to fail, learn from their failures, and try again. That environment must be realistic, presenting real-world problems that elicit real-world emotions. But it must also be safe, so that employees are not faced with real-world consequences for failure.

Simulations create this type of environment.

A good business simulation quickly turns existing knowledge into skills by providing a safe environment in which participants can practice.

Much like Red Flag, a business simulation allows employees to develop confidence by observing the effects their decisions and actions have on both specific areas of the business and on the business as a whole. In a well-designed and correctly-applied business simulation, employees learn without the risk of losing customer relationships, risking real resources, or jeopardizing real revenues.

When organizations invest in developing simulations as a primary learning method, training as we have know it gives way to intense real-world experiences designed to collapse the learning curve. These simulation experiences allow participants to make mistakes in a controlled environment and quickly apply what was learned to their jobs.

Executives love 'em

The most important benefit of simulations, in fact, is their power as effective executive tools to plan, project, and, most importantly, *engage* every employee in the "big picture" of the organization.

In the same Accenture study mentioned earlier, seventy-seven percent of executives surveyed said that they want their business' learning strategies to be aligned with their business goals. However, only eleven percent are satisfied with the progress their training departments are making to meet this need. The study also found that a mere twenty-six percent of C-Level respondents believed that three-quarters or more of their employees understand their company's strategic goals.

What does this all mean? Executives are consistently experiencing concerns that can be solved with business simulations!

Simulations help employees understand the "big picture." Unlike most training programs that focus on just one part of a business—such as sales, operations, or customer service—a simulation can model an entire business.

In his best-selling book *Good to Great*, Jim Collins found that two of the defining characteristics of a great company are its ability to find the right talent and to then focus everyone's attention on the task of creating a great company.[4] The difficulty in all this, of course, is getting great talent to play well together.

The Power of Simulations in Action

In 1994, Wayne Willis, president of the telecommunications company Voice-Tel Enterprises, participated in a two-day classroom-based sales simulation. During the simulation, Voice-Tel employees were divided into two mock companies that competed to sell communication services to one "customer."

Going into the simulation, Willis was skeptical about the likelihood of seeing real progress. But as he watched his sales reps immerse themselves completely in the experience, his attitude began to change.

During the simulation, Willis' employees became deeply involved in the sales process. In one team's workroom, an intense argument broke out regarding the best way to meet the customer's needs. In another room, three team members decided to work through the lunch hour in order to prepare a solution for the client. This wasn't ordinary training, Willis thought. In every way, it seemed like his employees were engaged in a real sales process.

By the second day of the simulation, Willis found himself caught up in the experience. The atmosphere was tense, the competition stiff, and out of all the contenders, Willis' team was one of only two finalists vying for the customer contract.

The last task of the simulation involved performing a business presentation to the "buyer." Willis had a flight scheduled for that afternoon; he had known going into the simulation that he would have to leave early and miss the last thirty minutes of class.

"I remember looking at my watch and thinking, 'I have to leave to catch the plane.' But I couldn't leave until I had heard the customer's full report. Had my team captured the account? We thought we had done an exceptional job, especially in the final round, but so had the other team. I was shocked when I saw the competitor's presentation. It had emphasized some areas my team had barely mentioned. Was the customer really that interested in the options for delivery that the other team emphasized? How important was the scalability of the solution to the customer, which we hadn't even touched upon in our presentation? Our team had not fully explored these areas and the competition had. I could not leave until I knew who had won the business."

As his plane prepared to take off without him, Willis discovered that his team had not won the contract. As disappointing as this was, Willis left with only positive feelings about the experience. "I will never forget the impact of the simulation and what we took away from it. There was a noticeable and immediate change in the depth and questioning that the sales reps did when they were back on the job the next week. We also tracked our sales after the simulation ended, and the increases we experienced were directly attributable to the simulation."

How did the simulation compare to past Voice-Tel sales training? "We had trained and trained on sales skills using role plays, round robins, and all of the traditional practice activities," says Willis. "That training helped, but it was nothing compared to mimicking the real-world experience of building a customer relationship over a series of phone calls, proposing and presenting, and, finally, finding out how we compared to the competition—and, of course, whether we won the contract or not."

To have a busy CEO miss his flight and delay other appointments because of a training simulation is quite a testament to just how engaging and successful simulations can be. Despite the fact that his team didn't win the "customer," Willis was the biggest winner of all in the end, as the skills that his employees gained as a result of participating in the simulation profoundly impacted the company's sales. Voice-Tel's follow-up studies showed that the sales employees who had gone through the simulation experience out-sold by more than seventy percent their colleagues who were not involved in the training.

Simulations bridge the gap

It's no longer sufficient for training departments to solve short-term problems; in today's market they need to be partners in developing and implementing corporate strategy.

In order to do that, training must not end with teaching skills; it must also demonstrate how those skills relate to operating the business and to executing business strategy. Only when employees really understand how their businesses work and how they fit into the bigger picture will training be successful.

Developing a strategic training initiative must be a joint effort between the executive team and the training department, each bringing their group's specific skills and motivations to the program. The training department specializes in assessing employees' current skills and identifying areas that need development. The executive team, meanwhile, identifies long-term strategy and direction for the company. The role of a business simulation is to bring these two capabilities together, to bridge the gap between where a company is now and where it wants to be. A simulation can only work if a company starts with a clear picture of where it is and where it wants to go.

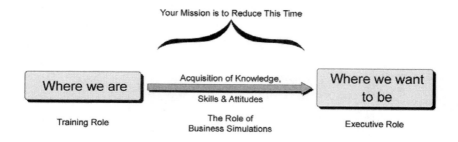

24

In addition to accomplishing traditional training objectives (such as imparting knowledge and developing skills), simulations have the potential to reach beyond merely "teaching" workers to strengthening overall organizations by building stronger, more cohesive teams, enhancing cross-departmental coordination and communication, and teaching workers the effects of their day-to-day decisions on the enterprise as a whole.

What Is a Business Simulation?

If you never have participated in a simulation, you may have trouble understanding what it is and how it works. Imagine the following scenario:

You and three other simulation participants have been appointed by your company's "board of directors" to take on a special project. The board explains that during the past year, the stock prices of each of your main competitors have increased by more than twenty percent, while your company's stock has remained flat. In order to better compete, the board challenges your team to achieve ten to fifteen percent annual growth in top-line revenue, EBITDA (Earnings Before Interest, Taxes, Depreciation, and Amortization), and stock price for each of the next three years.

In the first round, you receive information (sales figures, financial data, market research, consumer perception data, product supply chain data, etc.) to assist you in implementing the business strategy set by the board. Armed with information, you make strategic and operational decisions about pricing, advertising, operations, production, and new product development, all in an attempt to achieve your assigned goals.

Your team makes collective decisions and enters them through a website or other computer interface. The software behind the simulation imitates both your company and the market in which your company competes, using your decisions to calculate how markets move and how certain areas of the business are affected. The simulation then produces a new set of reports, market research, and performance indexes that show how your company is performing.

After each round, your team takes time to debrief and receive input on your overall performance. Did you increase market share? Did your profits go up or down? Did market awareness of your brands increase? How did your decisions in one area impact other aspects of your business? Did you make progress toward accomplishing the business challenge from the board?

You apply the lessons you learned in the first round in the next round of the simulation.

In this example, the business simulation allowed you to:

- Experiment with various parts of a business by making decisions about pricing, advertising, finance, operations, and new product development.
- Develop both a broad and a deep understanding of how the various parts of the business and various business processes depend on and affect each other.
- Apply and improve multiple skills: teamwork, data analysis, forecasting, decision-making, and critical thinking.
- Modify your thinking based on feedback provided by the simulation and by team debriefs.
- Create new skills, ideas, or approaches as a result of practicing within the simulation or through cross-training with other team members.
- Build confidence in your abilities.
- Learn to focus (that is, better understand the distinction between major issues and minor issues).

A business simulation creates an environment in which participants can actively acquire business operation knowledge, skills, and abilities. Most business simulations fall into one or more of these categories:

- Simulations that create an environment allowing participants to gain a deeper understanding of how their company or various parts of their company work.
- Simulations that model processes or tools, giving participants the opportunity to learn about and improve in these areas.
- Simulations that focus on developing knowledge and/or skills that can be applied to workplace tasks or situations.

Most business simulations focus on creating an environment in which participants can practice skills in an effort to implement a specific business *strategy*. These simulations *motivate* employees by modeling or mimicking the various *implementers* that influence a company's ability to implement a business strategy and achieve its goals. All simulations feature some form of *technology and tools* that guide learners through the simulated experience. Finally, all simulations feature an *environment* that defines the flow and structure of the simulation, as well as *content* that is used to help learners acquire new skills and knowledge. These components comprise the SIMTEC™ Model (Strategy, Implementers, Motivators, Technology and Tools, Environment, and Content). We will explore each of these concepts in more detail in Part Two.

For the purposes of this book, a business simulation is a training solution that contains SIMTEC and is used to create a learning solution that closely approximates a real-world business environment in order to help a company implement a business strategy designed to achieve a business goal. The real-world business environment mimicked by a business simulation encompasses all the tasks, systemic environments, and emotional and human interactions necessary to shorten the time it takes for workers to learn new skills and knowledge to implement the business strategy.

While many other definitions of simulations exist, sticking to the above definition will help you understand simulations and their purposes, why they work, what a business simulation typically includes, and, most importantly, their potential value to you and your business.

Why Simulations Work

"Practice, practice, and practice" isn't just the motto of the National Piano Teachers' Federation. Practice is the key to successful learning across disciplines and the centerpiece of a good simulation. Great coaches understand that in order to achieve maximum performance, a person's practice must consist of repeatable actions and unpredictable events. Repeatable actions reinforce skills; unpredictable events develop responsiveness and critical thinking.

> **Why Simulations Work**
> Simulations work because they allow learners to take the valuable knowledge and skills taught in books, e-learning, and the classroom, and practice applying them in an environment that closely approximates the real world. In addition, well-designed custom business simulations evoke emotions, parallel the learner's job, offer specific feedback from multiple sources, encompass predictable and unpredictable events, promote team interaction, and encourage creative decision-making and discovery.

Why are simulations so effective? For almost half a century, researchers have attempted to answer that very question. Studies have covered nearly every imaginable aspect of simulation-driven learning, including:

- Do simulations produce superior learning results compared to traditional learning techniques?
- Can success in simulations be attributed to luck rather than skill and effort?

- Does simulation performance correlate with learning?

Instead of being diminished by such scrutiny, simulations have proven time and time again that they are exceptional learning tools. Why? Simulations–unlike any other learning tool short of actual on-the-job, trial-and-error experience–*leverage the many different ways adults learn effectively.*

When simulations are used properly to challenge participants to practice multiple skills, they provide an environment in which most people learn effectively–through experience. Many studies have compared case method (books, case materials, and lectures) to learning by doing (simulations). The first study was done by A.P. Raia in 1966. He compared a business simulation named MANSYM to the equivalent strategic management course. He found that students who experienced MANSYM obtained higher learning levels than those who pursued the same senior-level case method course.[5]

It could be argued that the age of this study makes it irrelevant to the complex business simulations of today. However, Raia's findings merely set the tone for what future researchers would discover.

In 1975, Wolfe and Guth arrived at similar results. Using a privately published version of the Purdue Industrial Administration Decision Simulation, researchers concluded that "significant knowledge gains were obtained on seven of the nine questions posed for both [book and simulation] groups, though the game's learning outcomes were superior. These superior results emanated from the game's ability to produce greater advances in the knowledge of strategic management principles or concepts."[6]

White and Von Riesen more recently concluded that simulations have benefits beyond streamlining the training process. In a 1992 study they found that "satisfaction increased with simulation participation." Why? Perhaps the best reason can be explained by the work of McCarthy, who integrated the major findings of Kolb, Jung, Lotas, Fischer, Gregorc, Wetzig, and Merrill into four major learning styles:[7]

- **Style 1:** Learners perceive information concretely and process it reflectively, are divergent thinkers who believe in their own experience, excel in viewing concrete situations from many perspectives, model themselves on those they respect, learn by relating concepts to people, and are idea people.
- **Style 2:** Learners perceive information abstractly and process it reflectively, learn by thinking through ideas, collect and critique information, and need to know what the experts think.
- **Style 3:** Learners perceive information abstractly and process it actively, need hands-on experiences to know how things work, need to know how things they are asked to do apply to 'real life,' build concepts form factual data, and edit reality so they perceive only the information they see as relevant.
- **Style 4:** Learners perceive information concretely and process it actively, like variety and change, excel in situations calling for flexibility, like to take risks, and learn by trial and error and self-discovery

Business simulations are the only training solutions that incorporate all four learning styles. They succeed because there will be something in a simulation that fits each participant's learning style, no matter what that style is.

Experience makes the difference

Experience is critical to any business. Yet it may take a new manager six months or longer to learn about her new company and its operations, sales and marketing activities, human resources (HR) procedures, team dynamics, and so on.

Typically, the new manager learns about her job and her organization through exposure and inculcation–job-shadowing, training sessions, mentoring, participation in meetings, and talking with direct reports. During this time, she would both succeed and make mistakes, relying on expensive trial and error. By the time six months have passed, the new manager's experience, skills, and competencies make her an invaluable asset to her company.

If given the opportunity, however, most organizations would love to enjoy the benefits of the manager's hard-won knowledge, skills, and

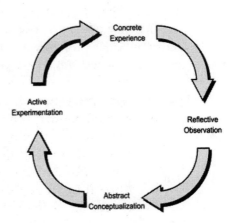

In the simplest terms, simulations focus on doing (experiencing) and then reflecting (thinking), then doing again. D.A. Kolb and R. Fry present an experiential "learning cycle" model that elaborates on this experiential dynamic.

experience sooner rather than later, without incurring the time and expense associated with training her over a long period. Experiential learning activities, of which simulations are a subset, allow companies to accomplish just this by accelerating the process, allowing the new manager to acquire the same knowledge, skills, and abilities that she would learn on the job in only days or weeks.

Lessons Learned

Many large private and public corporations have already started integrating simulations into their training programs and have realized significant improvements in employee performance as a result.

Humana Inc., a health insurance provider headquartered in Louisville, KY, recently used a simulation to quickly implement a new strategy for its managers. The results were astounding. "Only four months after the workshop," Chief

Learning Officer Ray Vigil says, "participants attributed savings that amount to an ROI of 14-to-1 directly to the program."[8]

It's no surprise that the results such simulations have generated are prompting other organizations to turn to simulations to meet their own training needs.

Value Propositions

Value propositions are a concept that businesses have embraced and use as a driving force to evaluate everything from strategies to resource allocation. A value proposition is the bundle of promises, both explicit and implicit, that a company makes to its customers about the cost, quality, and timeliness of its goods and services in exchange for their money. These are important to consider when analyzing both the costs associated with buying or building a simulation and the return on investment a simulation might deliver.

Simulations offer a number of value propositions to the three traditional primary stakeholders in company training programs: training managers, executives, and other business leaders and learning providers. Training managers always are on the lookout for learning solutions that develop multiple skills and quickly improve overall performance. Executives want the same thing—but they also want to be certain that the learning solution is tied to improving the business. Learning providers (e.g., training departments or external training vendors) look for solutions that they can develop cost-effectively and that also allow them to meet the goals of both the training managers and business leaders they serve.

Simulations meet the requirements of all three stakeholders:

- Business simulations accelerate performance improvement (or Speed to Performance).
- Business simulations serve as strategic initiative tools.

- Business simulations are viable learning solutions.

Accelerating Speed to Performance™

As we discussed earlier, one of the most attractive value propositions of simulations is their ability to shorten the time it takes to turn knowledge into skills. Accelerating Speed to Performance simply means that a learning solution is capable of reducing the cycle time (that is, the elapsed clock or calendar time from start to finish) that it takes for employees to convert new knowledge into skills.

Imagine, for example, that it typically takes an organization ten eight-hour workdays to train new call-center hires to do their jobs effectively and respond knowledgably to customer questions and to introduce them into the culture of the organization. In that case, a learning solution that reduces training cycle time from ten to seven days is desirable. Even more desirable, of course, would be a learning solution that could collapse the learning curve even more significantly—reducing cycle time from ten days to only five or four without any reduction or retention of skills.

Training managers, in particular, see a great deal of value in simulations because of the many skills they force learners to apply and practice. Instead of concentrating on one specific skill for a period of time, simulations force participants to practice several skills at once. This effect accelerates Speed to Performance by allowing trainees to use familiar skills as a base on which to build new knowledge and skills. Simulations also afford participants an opportunity to keep old and/or seldom-used skills fresh.

How else, specifically, do business simulations accelerate Speed to Performance? They teach employees valuable real-world skills, including how to:

- set and achieve goals
- receive and give feedback

- focus on the major issues and not the irrelevant or minor issues
- deal with interruptions and distractions
- work individually and collaborating in teams
- explore alternative options
- deal with stress
- have fun

Each benefit is explained below, and will be covered in more detail in Part 2. These experiences are important to training managers and executives alike, because they reinforce the application of multiple skills and the practice of new skills with the goal of accelerating Speed to Performance. Additionally, these experiences all contribute to the realism of a simulation. They pull participants into the experience, allowing them to take an important and active role in running a company.

Set and achieve goals–Businesspeople are goal-oriented. Research shows that those with clearly defined goals tend to earn $3,000 to $5,000 more per month, are healthier, and live more balanced lives. Goals provide motivation, direction, and reward. Goals also serve as guides; they let us know whether we're on the right track. Business simulations leverage this power by giving participants the opportunity to set and achieve goals threaded throughout the simulation.

Receive and give feedback–In the business world, feedback comes in many different forms. Financial statements and management reports provide a glimpse into overall company performance. End-of-year performance reviews give us insight into individual opportunities for improvement. Managers, peers, and employees provide both verbal and non-verbal feedback. External resources such as market reports and industry news influence our decision-making.

All of this feedback is crucial. Research shows, in fact, that the "most powerful single moderator that enhances achievement is *feedback*."[9] Feedback allows us to accurately evaluate ourselves and make changes when we need to do so.

Feedback is a crucial part of a high-impact business simulation because it both challenges learners to examine the cause-and-effect relationship between decisions and their outcomes and expands learners' abilities to solve complex problems. Learning how to evaluate and react to feedback is a critical business skill. It is no wonder, then, that simulations that incorporate several feedback elements accelerate learning and guide learners to achieve performance targets.

Focus on the majors and not the minors–The ability to filter information–eliminating the noise and focusing only on what's important–is a crucial skill for success in any business. Simulations develop learners' abilities to do just this by showing them to use information wisely.

Deal with interruptions and distractions–Can you remember a time when you were able to focus completely on one task from the time you started it until the time you completed it? Probably not. For most of us, uninterrupted time is a luxury rarely enjoyed. Interruptions are a regular part of the real world, and they're an integral part of a business simulation. Simulations employ interruptions in order to force learners to spread their focus among multiple tasks and prioritize activities according to urgency and importance.

Explore alternative options–One of the problems with the real world is that we can only make one decision at a time. We might like a chance to try out different options, but by the time we have seen the results of one decision, it often is too late to try something else. This has led to the popularity of "What if" questioning in business circles, which often is an exercise in futility in the real world.

But simulations are different. In fact, one of the most important elements of a simulation is its ability to allow learners to ask and answer "What if?" questions. In an effective simulation, learners can explore different options, make various decisions, and observe how the business might react, all without the risk of "real world" implications.

Work within teams–According to Carl Larson, author of *Team Excellence* and *What Makes Teams Work*, cooperative learning is one of the most effective tools for accelerating learning. When people collaborate in teams, he says, they learn more quickly than they ever would working alone. In addition to giving learners the chance to ask questions and discuss problems with others, working in teams within a simulation also allows participants to gain new perspectives and develop important real-world interpersonal communication skills.

Deal with stress–The business environment is fast-paced, ever-changing, and often stressful. New contracts, lost customers, the need to exceed shareholder expectations, and continual high-stakes decision-making add to the daily drama and tension of the business world. Amidst all this chaos, information and events do not flow linearly through time. Workflow and human interactions are not neat and predictable. We constantly filter various inputs and react to situations. All of these factors increase tension in the real world and explain why tension is a key part of an effective simulation.

Incorporating tension into a simulation increases learner engagement and deepens the learning experience because a healthy level of tension improves our memory and thus our ability to learn. When we experience anxiety and fear, our brains release hormones as part of the fight-flight syndrome to prepare us for action. During this heightened emotional state, the likelihood that an experience will make a lasting imprint in our memory doubles.

Have fun–Almost any child would rather play a game than sit in a classroom. The same holds true for adults. Simulations are often compared to games, which is a good way to think about them. Games, after all, by their very nature provide motivation, structure, and goals. They also create a competitive environment for learning.

It is important to note that a business simulation can include gaming elements without becoming a "game"–and that simulations that include gaming elements such as scorekeeping, competition, and surprise variables can increase the entertainment value, fun, and *effectiveness* of a simulation.

Tools for strategic execution

Business simulations often are viewed as strategic execution tools because executive teams are often the ones sponsoring the activity in order to accelerate change within an organization and provide employees with a "big picture" understanding of their role in corporate strategy.

There are several reasons that executives consider simulations to be a valuable part of their toolkits:

See the big picture–A good training program will relate to a company's overall strategy and mission. Unfortunately, most training programs never make these connections. Even after a great inspirational program, most employees leave training without a clear idea of how their business unit, their team, and their individual jobs actually impact execution of the business' strategy and goals. In fact, at most companies, the majority of employees don't even know what the business strategies and goals are. This lack of strategic connection is a key reason most executives bemoan the lack of impact training has on the execution of strategy.

By contrast, a simulation that is motivated by and based on a carefully selected business strategy provides executives and other stakeholders with the confidence of knowing that employees will be immersed in the organization's strategy, and that they will have every opportunity to understand it and–in some instances–even improve it.

Seeing the Big Picture
Early one morning, a man was walking to work and passed three bricklayers beginning to work on a wall. The

naturally curious man watched each worker closely, and he noticed that there seemed to be significant differences in the quality of workmanship.

That evening, on his way home, the man passed the same three bricklayers and wondered again at how workers using the same brick and mortar could produce such different results.

The first bricklayer had about five rows of brick laid for his portion of the wall. He was slapping down the mortar and placing it on the bricks. He seemed far more interested in what was playing on his headphones than he was in his work. The man asked him what he was building, and the bricklayer responded, "I am laying bricks. I am a bricklayer; surely you can see that."

The second bricklayer had built his part of the wall to about shoulder height. The bricks were even, and the bricklayer set them carefully and made sure the mortar was even before moving to the next section. The man asked the second bricklayer what he was building, and the bricklayer paused before he replied, "Why, I am building a wall. It is going to be a large and tall wall, so the bricks need to be just so in order to support it."

The third bricklayer was already on scaffolding. Although his portion of the wall was more than twelve feet high, he placed his bricks quickly and carefully. His wall looked flawless, smooth, and almost a work of art.

More curious than ever, the man went to the third bricklayer and asked his question. "Excuse me, sir, what are you building?"

The bricklayer stopped and looked down. "Well," he said, "I'm laying bricks that will build the wall of a great cathedral. It's going to be a place where people come to worship and pray. It will stand here for hundreds of years, so my bricks have to be perfect."

Build critical-thinking skills—What's every executive's dream? To have employees who are capable of skillfully conceptualizing, analyzing, and synthesizing information from various sources, and improving their decisions and actions based on that information.

Critical thinking at this level is a difficult skill to teach using traditional training methods. Simulations, however, provide an excellent framework for developing critical-thinking skills. The organic, explorative, trial-and-error characteristics of simulations present employees with a vast array of information. As participants work within a simulation to analyze the data, make decisions based on it, and then evaluate the consequences of their decisions and actions, they begin to develop the critical-thinking skills that executives covet.

Create focused teams—According to Dr. Carl Larson, author of *When Teams Work Best: 6,000 Team Members and Leaders Tell What It Takes to Succeed* and *Teamwork: What Must Go Right/What Can Go Wrong,* managers spend twenty-five to forty percent of their time dealing with issues among team members.[10] Larson also says that team learning is one of the most effective types of accelerated learning. When people collaborate in teams, he says, they learn more and they learn it more quickly than they ever would alone.

Given the fact that many business simulations are run in team environments, these tools are an excellent vehicle for getting people to work with others and share knowledge with each other.

Leverage best practices—Ever try to extend a best practice outside the group that created it? It's not easy. At best, you may think of a clever acronym or slogan that gets printed on posters, mouse pads, and perhaps even a few t-shirts or coffee mugs, but the actual behaviors you try to instill rarely are adopted by others in the organization.

Why is this? Best practices are created through trial-and-error, and they work well because the people who use them are the people who discovered them. A simulation can help transfer best practices. Instead of documenting the process and procedures, a simulation can challenge participants to discover best practice themselves.

Viable learning solutions

Business simulations today are viable learning solutions because the costs associated with building and maintaining them have dropped dramatically.

Only a few years ago, simulations often were considered too expensive, too difficult to implement due to immature technology, and too costly to maintain. That is no longer the case. Recent developments have changed each of those perceptions, prompting more and more organizations to add simulations to their repertoires.

Less expensive to build–For decades, simulations remained out of reach to all but the wealthiest organizations. In the 1980s, a full custom business simulation could cost millions of dollars, making simulations impractical as training tools. Recent technological advances and increased competition by existing and emergent simulation vendors, however, have lowered the price of custom and off-the-shelf simulations significantly.

Just how precipitously have prices fallen in recent years? James Lundy, a vice president at the Stamford, CT research firm Gartner Inc., offered this example in a recent *Computer World* article: "A couple of years ago, you might have been talking $200,000 for an hour-long course. Today, using still shots instead of custom video, you're talking $20,000."[11]

Technological advancements– Perhaps the single most important factor contributing to the increased use, affordability, and availability of simulations is the advancement of technology. Everything from high-speed Internet access to faster processors, rapid-authoring tools to increased computer memory and better software, has contributed directly to the increased pervasiveness of simulations.

Technological advancements also have decreased the time it takes build complex business simulations. A simulation modeling multiple business operations and processes, for example, once took Regis Learning Solutions a year to develop. Today, the same simulation takes only four to six months.

Easier to maintain—In today's business world, it isn't enough to be the best company in your town, state, or country. Today, nearly every company competes on a global playing field and faces increasing pressure and competition from companies around the globe.

With this increased competition comes the need to move faster and, as a result, increased pressure for good, quick, effective training -- training that makes employees better than those of their competitors, no matter where the competitors may be located. To achieve this goal, simulations have to be relatively easy to maintain. And because business realities are constantly shifting, they must be simple to update over time.

Administration, facilitation, and maintenance of simulations have become easier in order to meet this need. Companies like Management Simulation Inc., for example, offer universities on-line simulations that include administrative tools allowing a single professor to facilitate, administer, and maintain the simulation.

Why Have Organizations Been Slow to Adopt Simulations?

Business simulations provide legitimate value propositions for training managers, business leaders, and learning providers. Regardless of these value propositions, however, many organizations have been slow to adopt simulations.

Why is this? For most of the past fifty years, business simulations primarily have existed only in universities, primarily business schools. Today, in fact, 97.5 percent of Association to Advance Collegiate Schools of Business (AACSB) members use business simulations as part of their curriculum.[12] Traditionally, these schools could afford to invest the time, energy, and money necessary to create high-impact simulations, because little of their content would change over time; a simulation could be created once and then used and reused again—sometimes for decades.

For the most part, however, organizations immersed in the fast-paced, rapidly changing environment of real-world business have remained reluctant to adopt simulations for training purposes. Until recently, this made sense. Expensive, complicated, and time-consuming simulations probably wouldn't have been the best way for time-strapped, cost-conscious organizations to train employees.

Today, business simulations truly do improve performance faster than most other types of learning interventions, and so it now makes sense to invest in them. However, it's still all too easy for organizations to under- or over-develop a simulation or purchase one that is more complex or expensive than necessary.

Simulations Are More Than a Training Solution

Don't position a simulation as a "training solution" when selling it to senior executives. To most executives, a simulation is not a "training tool." It is an environment that helps employees view the company from a "big picture" perspective, understand organizational goals and strategies, and apply new skills and knowledge.

How This Book Will Help

If businesses truly are to capitalize on simulations in the years to come, they need a guide for keeping costs in check and ensuring that the simulations they implement are neither too much nor too little for their needs. In short, businesses need a guide.

This book is intended to serve as that guide. Regis Learning Solutions has emerged as one of the leading innovators in utilizing business simulations, and we are eager to share our experiences and knowledge to serve large and small companies still struggling to communicate business strategy and vision to employees.

On the following pages you will find models, tools, tips, best practices, and case studies to help guide the selection and development process for business simulations. Of equal importance, the book also explains when a simulation is appropriate and when it is not.

We hope we not only provide a framework for understanding the various features that a business simulation may include, but also provide advice on how to incorporate the appropriate elements into your own simulation. Too many businesses buy into the hype mentioned earlier, and under- or over-develop, or buy a business simulation that is too complex, or pay too much money for what they need. We don't want that to happen to you.

---

[1] Adkins, Sam S. "The 2002- 2010 U.S. Market for E-Learning Industry: The Shape of the Next Generation E-Learning Market." 2002. Brandon Hall.com.   15   July   2005   <http://www.brandonhall.com/public/publications/market-sim/index.htm)>.

[2] Hebert, Adam J. "Red Flag With a Difference." *Air Force Magazine Online* 88   (2005):   6   pages.   24   Oct.   2005   <http://www.afa.org/magazine/Aug2005/0805redflag.asp>

[3] Pfeffer, Jeffrey and Robert I. Sutton. *The Knowing-Doing Gap: How Smart Companies Turn Knowledge into Action.* Boston: Harvard Business School Press, 2000.

[4] Collins, Jim. *Good to Great: Why Some Companies Make the Leap… and Others Don't.* New York: Harper Business, 2001.

[5] Wolfe, Joseph and Denise Luethge. "The Impact of Involvement on Performance in Business Simulations: An examination of Goosen's 'Know Little' Decision- Making Thesis." *Journal of Education for Business,* Nov / Dec. 2003.

[6] Ibid.

[7] McCarthy, Bernice. 4MAT System: Teaching to Learning Styles with Right-Left Mode Techniques. New York: Excel Inc, 1980.

[8] Boehle, Sarah. "The Next Generation of E-Learning." Training Jan. 2005: 23 -31.

[9] Hattie, John, and Richard Jaeger. "Assessment and Classroom learning: A deductive approach." Assessment in Education: Principles, Policy & Practice 5.1 (1998): 111- 23.

[10] Larson, Carl, and Frank M.J. LaFasto. When Teams Work Best: 6,000 Team Members and Leaders Tell What It Takes to Succeed. Thousand Oaks, CA: SAGE Publications, 2001.

[11] Hoffman, Thomas. "Simulations Revitalize E-Learning: E-learning Simulation Frameworks have Become Cheaper and Easier to Deploy." 2004. Computer World.com. 6 July 2005 <http://www.computerworld.com/ careertopics/ careers/training/story/ 0,10801,83639,00.html>.

[12] Summers, Gary J. "Today's Business Simulation Industry." Simulation & Gaming 35.2 (2004): 208–41.

2

PART TWO:

UNDERSTANDING BUSINESS SIMULATIONS

A great company—one that expects and elicits exceptional performance from its employees—understands that workers must not only be able to effectively execute tactics in support of a strategy, they also must understand how their actions and decisions contribute to the implementation of the business strategy and, ultimately, the achievement of overall corporate goals.

In Part One, we examined why business simulations are so successful in communicating corporate strategy. Part Two will take that knowledge and apply it to your own situation, offering guidelines and information to help you find the training solution that is best for your organization.

There are simulations for nearly every timeframe, budget, and business need. In fact, many companies find that the hardest part isn't deciding to use a simulation; it's narrowing down the choices and picking the one that makes the most sense for their situation.

While we were writing this book, the RLS staff tried for months to build a table listing all the types of simulations in existence. We eventually decided that it was impossible to compile a complete list; new programs are created all the time. So instead of a comprehensive list, we began to develop a comprehensive model we call SIMTEC, which provides a framework for understanding the key requirements of all business simulations.

The SIMTEC Model

As technology advances and the simulation market expands, the number of simulations available to businesses will continue to multiply. That's great news for those of us in the training industry, but more options bring more confusion.

How do you select a simulation? Which type of simulation is best for your company? Which features do you need? Can simulations really model the real world? What decisions need to be made regarding technology, tools, and content in the creation of your simulation environment? There are no easy answers, but working through these questions and more on the following pages will help you determine what kind of simulation will be best for your unique needs.

The SIMTEC model is a framework Regis Learning Solutions developed to understand and address these questions and others. Based on the belief that learning objectives need to align with company goals, the SIMTEC model serves both as a checklist for choosing and a blueprint for designing simulations.

At the center of the model is the business Strategy. All decisions regarding a business simulation drive toward addressing your business strategy, starting with the Implementers—which define how to execute the Strategy—and the Motivators, which define how to engage participants. These first three dimensions determine the overall goals and structure of the simulation.

The first three parts of the SIMTEC model must be followed in order. The Strategy must be identified first, followed by the Implementers, and then the Motivators. The Implementers and Motivators will drive the design of the 'TEC' (Technology and Tools, Environment, and Content) part of the model. Because the final three dimensions interrelate (a decision in one dimension will affect another dimension) it does not matter as much where you start. Ultimately, as the model shows, broad requirements (outer circle) will gradually refine toward the Strategy.

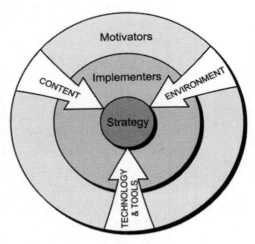

As we go through the SIMTEC model in the following pages, we will explore how two real organizations used it to identify business Strategies, define and select key Implementers, Motivate participants, and create a simulation using Technology and Tools, Environment, and Content dimensions as guides. The first case study provides an example of a classroom-based sales simulation. The second demonstrates how the model was used to create an on-line simulation.

2.1 STRATEGY

Successful corporations are goal-driven. For example, Microsoft Corporation founder Bill Gates' famous goal of putting "a computer on every desk and in every home" helped him to grow his organization from a small software startup to its current status as one of the largest companies in the world.[13]

Gates didn't just rely on setting a goal, though. He didn't send an e-mail to his employees expressing his vision and then let it go. Instead, he put together some very specific strategies and focused the most talented minds of his company on executing those strategies. He recognized that companies depend on strategies and specific action plans to accomplish the goals that set them apart from their competition.

Like Bill Gates, other great executives–including Jack Welch, Sam Walton, Meg Whitman, and Warren Buffet–understand the importance of ensuring that employees both clearly understand the company's goals and the plans to achieve them, and that they have the skills to successfully execute them. Without the right skills, execution is not possible and goals are rarely achieved.

There are, however, common barriers to an employee's successful execution of business strategies, regardless of the executive's desire. These include:

- Employees don't possess the skills or knowledge to implement a strategy effectively (or implement the tactics that make up the strategy).
- Employees don't understand how the strategy relates to the business goal.
- Employees don't understand how their roles contribute to the strategy.
- Employees don't understand how one strategy impacts another in support of the same business goal.

- Employees' motivations to implement the strategy are inadequate.
- Communication among individuals and teams is poor.
- Inadequate processes impede workers' efforts to implement a strategy effectively.

The Executive Nightmare

Everyone was excited! The executive team presented a powerful vision for a new product–the super widget. The super widget was amazing, destined to spur a real product revolution that certainly would set the company apart from their competition.

Energized and enthusiastic, employees went back to their desks to begin developing their strategies to bring the widget to market. After the strategies were defined, project managers worked all weekend to create masterful project plans outlining exactly how implementation of the strategy would work and how each employee team would contribute to the implementation.

Three months into the project, the executive team checked in with their employees. "On target and on budget," the teams reported. Six months into the project, the leaders checked in again. "We're on target and on budget!"

Executives were happy with the results, and they began to generate buzz in the market.

Then the bad news came. With only forty-five days left until the planned release of the super widget, team leaders said, "We're way off target and about $3 million over budget."

Great companies realize that the key to successful execution of corporate strategy depends on their employees' ability to understand how their actions impact that strategy.

Most often, goals (e.g. to become a market share leader) of an organization are set by the executive team, who then share the vision with management–usually through simple PowerPoint presentations or corporate memos. Management, in turn, authors specific strategies (e.g. to increase customer loyalty and release new products) for accomplishing the goal.

These strategies then are presented to employees (again, typically through PowerPoint presentations or via e-mail), who in turn focus on the tactical aspects of implementing the direction. These employees work tirelessly to perform their assigned tasks—hopefully believing that their actions will contribute in some way to helping the company achieve its goal.

It doesn't always work out well. Managers focused only on their individual areas of the organization often feel disconnected from the overall corporate goal. They fail to understand or appreciate how their strategies ultimately impact achievement of a goal. Employees, for their part, may be in an even worse position. Focused primarily on tactical matters and day-to-day operations and challenges, they often are too far removed from the goals they are supposedly working to support, and they fail to understand how their own individual actions influence the bigger picture. And yet executives stay awake at night worrying that employees might innocently take an action that seriously damages the organization's strategic execution.

When this scenario occurs, the "Executive Nightmare" described in the story of the super widgets is too often the reality. Everyone works hard, but only a few executives have a clear idea of what they're working toward.

A great company—a company that expects and elicits exceptional performance from its employees—understands that workers must not only perform in support of a strategy effectively, but they also must understand *how* their actions and decisions contribute to the implementation of business strategy and, ultimately, the achievement of overall corporate goals.

The purpose of a business simulation is to create an environment in which employees can develop the skills they need to execute the company's strategies. In a simulation, employees examine their assumptions, assess different circumstances, link strategies to operations, and evaluate results. At the same time, they're challenged to re-evaluate everything they believe they understand.

The Simulation Decision Tree

The first key to training success is deciding whether a business simulation will help you implement your strategy. The following Simulation Decision Tree, which is a component of the SIMTEC model, outlines a three-step process to ensure that a simulation will help your organization implement its strategy.

There are a number of established performance models designed to help training professionals analyze an array of performance problems and determine appropriate solutions.

Robert Mager and Peter Pipe's Performance Analysis Flow Diagram[14] and Dana and James Robinson's Performance Relationship Map[15] are just two examples. Both are excellent general performance models that, with many others, influenced the creation of our own Decision Tree.

RLS created the Simulation Decision Tree because the unique characteristics of business simulations require a specific tool to help companies choose the right one. Having a one-size-fits-all model for evaluation can lead to vague interpretation and selection of inappropriate interventions. The Simulation Decision Tree, by contrast, addresses the specific and unique issues you are likely to encounter as you address the Strategy component of SIMTEC.

The Decision Tree will help you identify your business strategy and decide whether or not a simulation is the best solution for developing your employees to implement that strategy. It will also challenge you to think through and categorize the type of intervention necessary to implement your strategy (learning vs. non-learning solution) and determine the performance level (awareness, literacy, fluency, mastery, or anticipatory).

Like all established performance models, the tree provides opportunities to select non-instructional interventions. This is intentional. Simulations are not necessary for many business strategies. In fact, more often than not, other solutions–from work-environment support to motivational programs and beyond–will suffice.

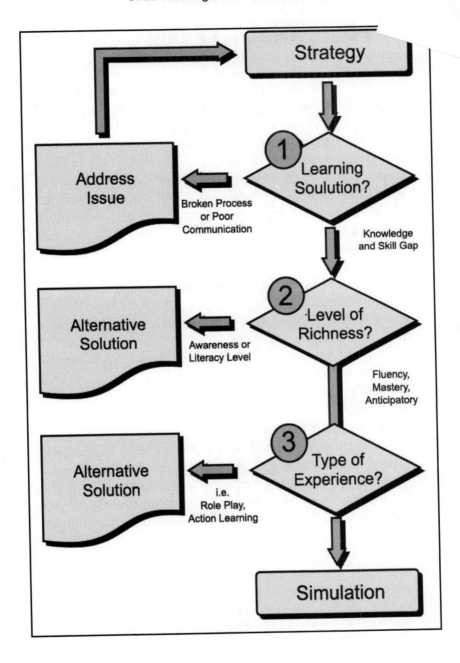

Step 1: Which learning solution will help you implement your strategy?

As we have said, training departments too often implement learning solutions without a clear idea of how the training relates to the business strategy.

Consider a company faced with poor customer-satisfaction ratings and declining market share. Their business goal seems clear: they need to find a way to improve the way their customers perceive them. Their strategy, therefore, should involve identifying and acting upon ways to improve those ratings.

Implementing a cohesive strategy, however, can be more difficult. Depending on their roles within the organization, managers will have different opinions regarding the strategy. A marketing manager might view lack of advertising dollars as the problem. "If we get a larger budget, we could develop a marketing campaign that could reach more people," he might reason. "As a result, we will increase our brand awareness and increase our positive visibility in the market."

An operations manager, meanwhile, might view the data as a production or inventory problem. "If we could make our production lines more efficient and increase our inventory so we have more products readily available," she might think, "we make our customers happier."

For his part, a sales manager might view the data and respond to it by suggesting that new product or service offerings should be added in order to better serve customers' evolving needs.

Can training actually help these individuals? At first glance, it appears that the solution that each manager recommended may better be addressed by improving a process or defining clearer communication channels. That's why the first step in the Decision Tree, from the training department's perspective, is to ensure that a learning solution will help workers to implement a particular strategy.

Simulations are impressive and highly effective, but like all learning solutions, they are not necessarily the answer for everything. Business strategies that merely require a company to improve employee motivation, re-engineer a process, or enhance communication can be implemented with non-learning interventions.

If you are trying to accomplish any of these three things, a simulation is not an appropriate intervention and you should stop your journey through the Decision Tree here. The best training program—simulation or otherwise—will not help you implement your strategy when the cause of a problem you are attempting to address is lack of motivation, poor communication, or lack of adequate process.

Determining if a Learning Solution Is Needed

Here's a simple litmus test for determining whether a learning solution will help you implement your business strategy.

If employees could perform a task or action associated with implementing strategy "if their lives depended on it," then they likely possess the necessary skills or knowledge to perform, but are not doing so for some other reason. In this instance, your root cause likely is a motivation, communication, or process issue that should be solved with a non-learning solution.

If employees could *not* perform the task or action associated with implementing company strategy if their lives depended on it, then a skill or knowledge gap likely exists, and a learning solution, such as a simulation or other intervention, is probably appropriate.

Consider this example:

Commercial Enterprises (CE) has three call centers where approximately two hundred employees are responsible for helping the company's customers. After doing a budget analysis, CE realized that the cost of marketing and recovering lost customers increased five percent over the previous year.

55

Why? CE offered a better product than its competitors, but many customers voiced frustration over the quality of CE's customer service. The competition was successfully taking away many of the unhappy customers.

CE quickly established a business goal (to improve customer service) and implemented a strategy (helping the company's call-center employees become more empathic and solution-oriented). The strategy, the company reasoned, would help it retain more customers and reduce costs associated with recovering customers who switched to competitor organizations.

In order to effectively implement its strategy, the company decided to offer more training to its customer-service team. However, at the time CE provided financial rewards to their customer-service representatives based on the total number of calls a person could react to per hour. The customer-service representatives were highly motivated to "fix" issues quickly, not completely. Thus, no matter how much training CE tossed at its reps, there was no way to create more empathetic, solution-oriented staff while continuing to reward quantity over quality.

The lesson? Before deciding to implement a specific kind of training program, consider whether non-learning interventions will suffice. In CE's case, further investigation made it abundantly clear to the company that it needed to change its reward and allow representatives more flexibility to do their jobs. Without changing this policy, no amount of training would help the company. If anything, training would only send conflicting messages to the customer-service representatives ("Keep call times down but be empathetic at the same time.")

If the strategy can be implemented by improving a process, establishing better communication procedures, or changing the motivational structure, do that first. More often than not, strategy implementation requires changes in at least one of these areas first, before a learning solution can be used to teach and reinforce the changes. If it's clear that a learning solution is ultimately needed, then move to step 2.

Step 2: What level of richness will your learning solution require?

If you have gotten this far, you have decided that a learning solution will help you implement your business strategy. Does this mean that implementing a simulation is your next step? Not quite.

Before selecting any learning intervention, determine the desired level of performance (or richness) employees will need to achieve in order to implement the business strategy.

Performance Level	At this level employees:
Awareness	▪ Recall essential principles, concepts, and vocabulary.
Literacy	▪ Discuss and explain basic concepts and vocabulary. ▪ Connect basic concepts to their daily work tasks.
Fluency	▪ Apply and implement knowledge and skills related to their daily work tasks quickly and efficiently. ▪ Explain basic concepts, principles, and vocabulary to others.
Mastery	▪ Perform at the fluency level. ▪ Solve unusual challenges and deftly apply skills and knowledge to both ordinary and extraordinary tasks.

Anticipatory	▪ Perform at the mastery level.
	▪ Foresee changes, problems, and the impact of trends and take actions to minimize their impact.
	▪ Foresee opportunities to leverage change to the organization's advantage.

Understanding where you are and where you want to go is critical to developing a learning solution. Eventually, you'll need to answer the questions, "Can a traditional learning solution solve our problems? Can it improve performance to the level the business requires quickly enough to meet our goal?"

On average, sixty percent of all corporate initiatives fail. Of those that succeed, most exceed their budgets. A major contributor to failed or over-budget projects is lack of experience. Reading about how to run a project from a manual is not enough. Understanding the process of how to take a product to market does not make a person a Product Manager.

For example, imagine that you have a team that needs to roll out a new product within six months. The team understands the process of product rollout, but no one has actually gone through the process from concept to delivery.

Examine the gap between the current and target performance levels for the product rollout and the time necessary to gain the know-how and confidence. Determine if a traditional learning solution will close the gap.

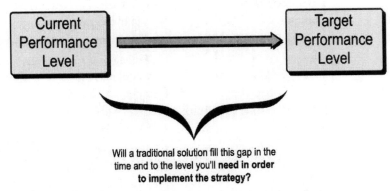

Will a traditional solution fill this gap in the
time and to the level you'll **need in order
to implement the strategy?**

If implementing your strategy requires employees to achieve only an awareness level of proficiency, a simulation is probably unnecessary. It would be difficult to justify incurring the costs and investing the time necessary to develop or purchase an experientially-focused simulation when less expensive, less time-consuming traditional solutions—such as classroom lectures, e-learning, or workbooks—can provide employees with the target level of awareness.

However, if you are tasked with moving employees to a mastery level of knowledge and skills or beyond, an experiential solution may be a good decision.

Step 3: What type of experiential solution is appropriate?

There is a simple way to identify whether an experiential solution is necessary.

As we have discussed, adults learn best through practice. As you think about the skills that your employees need to move from their current performance levels to the new levels, consider whether those skills can be acquired and fully understood through a method other than practice. In other words, will your employees be able to understand and apply these skills without being on the job for a period of time, practicing, making mistakes, and refining their skills?

To ensure that the skill you identify can be effectively taught through a simulation, determine if the skill can be

59

measured. If you see the skill performed, could you provide feedback on what worked and what did not work?

The primary benefit of determining what kind of learning solution you need is one of cost. If you don't need a simulation, then it's obviously better to invest your dollars in a more appropriate, cost-effective solution. However, it's imperative that you think realistically about what it will take to effectively apply acquired skills to the jobs you want your employees to do. Implementing the wrong solution will not only waste money; it will also waste time, fail to improve productivity, and cause you to fall short of your target performance levels.

Remember, executives are looking for solutions that produce fast results. Stop-gap training initiatives, used year after year, may create the illusion of action, but they will not produce the results necessary to achieve the business strategies.

In the previous step of the Simulation Decision Tree, we discussed the importance of knowing where you are and where you want to go. Once you know those things, you need to be realistic about whether the skills you need to get there can be acquired through any method other than through a simulated environment. You can use the following checklist to guide your thinking.

Do the skills required to execute your organization's strategy:

- Require workers to create a "mental map" or expert's model of how the business strategy works (in other words, a map of the path they must follow in order to implement the business strategy)?
- Require that workers apply multiple skills that have either direct or indirect impact on their ability to effectively implement the strategy?
- Require workers to understand how the application of multiple Implementers impacts successful execution of the strategy over a long period of time? (If so, in order for the workers to understand the cause-and-

effect relationship between their decisions and actions and the outcomes of those decisions and actions over time, they'll need to "simulate" time.)

- Require extensive practice in a real-world-like environment in order to learn new skills?

If you checked all of the items on the list, then a simulation is the right solution for your need.

It's All About Experience

A company with flat revenue over several quarters decides to focus on increasing revenue. To accomplish this goal, the company chooses to provide additional training to it sales team.

The training department identifies various tactics to implement their strategy. The first is to teach the sales reps how to "solution sell." Instead of simply taking orders, the idea goes, salespeople who understand customer needs and issues will be able to create solutions (a combination of products and services) to better serve their clients. The company believes that implementing this tactic will increase the size of contracts and thus increase revenue.

Another tactical focus is to teach employees to cross-sell. If the sales reps sell additional products to existing customers, they will widen the customer's reliance on the company and decrease the likelihood of the customer switching to a competitor. Implementing this approach will bring in new revenue and also reduce the cost of sales.

The business goal is apparent, the strategy logical, and the tactics are clear. The sales representatives target performance level—fluency with solution selling and cross-selling—is clear. However, the company's training professionals must still determine what type of experiential learning solution will be effective, and that is not clear.

Ask any top-performing salesperson how he learned to do his job, and he will tell you that understanding when to apply certain skills is an art form. Often you must "naturally" move between different strategies based on a customer's verbal

---

and non-verbal responses. But there are learned skills necessary for successful selling. You need to have a mental map of how to implement strategies. You need to understand how skills interrelate and when to apply them. Most sales take time, and different skills are applied at different times.

Therefore, the business that wants to further train its sales force needs to understand the cause-and-effect relationship between applying one skill at one point and its impact on its team's ability to apply another skill at another point. Simulations provide exactly this level of fluency with the benefit of experience.

Won't role plays, decision-making exercises, debate exercises, critique/evaluation exercises, game show format exercises, or other experiential learning solutions work? No, because other experiential learning programs do not address all the items on the checklist. They may do a great job at one or two of the items, but a simulation is the only option that will not only address all of the needs expressed, but it will demonstrate the interdependencies between the items.

Case Studies

At the end of each section, we will present information about two real-life cases to provide examples of how the SIMTEC model has been applied to real training problems. The first case illustrates how the SIMTEC model was used to gather requirements and design a three-day, fast-paced, facilitator-led simulation for a successful electronics distribution company. The second case, from a private university, involved the development of a team-based, on-line simulation. By demonstrating the two extremes, a purely facilitated simulation and a purely on-line simulation, we hope it will be clear how easy it is to apply the SIMTEC model to everything in between.

> **International Electronics Company (IEC)**
> **STRATEGY**

COMPANY HISTORY

ICE is a global leader in electronics distribution, headquartered in the Midwest. Its expansive global distribution network can reach ninety-nine percent of the world's major markets within forty-eight hours. IEC employs more than 5,600 people worldwide, including 2,000 technically trained salespeople who work in more than thirty languages.

CHALLENGES AND ISSUES

Recently, IEC underwent a significant reorganization and cost containment process, from which it emerged stronger and more focused.

When the reorganization began, IEC faced increased turnover in its sales department, longer lead-times to train new sales hires, and a need to quickly familiarize sales representatives with "cross-selling" by encouraging them to focus on selling products and services that would meet an array of customer needs.

Previously, IEC had run a ten-day training program for new sales representatives. This program taught new employees about the company's products and service offerings primarily through lecture, e-learning, and reading-based solutions focused on the rapid dissemination of a diverse body of knowledge. During the course, employees were expected to master everything from the gauge of copper wire in telephony products to the way to input orders using the company's sales and management tools. The ten-day program was intense for participants and too full of information, focused mostly on technical products and services rather than sales training.

When the reorganization began, senior management assessed the efficiency of the sales training program and ultimately decided to put it on hold. They identified skills not covered by the program that salespeople would need in order for IEC to effectively compete and grow. Specifically, the company's strategic goal was to change the sales culture from one that concentrated on "order taking" to one that focused on the identification of opportunities that would lead to additional sales through cross-selling and consultative and solution selling. This strategy was part of a bigger goal to increase customer satisfaction and, as a result, overall sales revenue.

APPLYING THE SIMULATION DECISION TREE

In order to achieve the strategic goal, IEC's leadership agreed that new employees needed a mastery-level understanding of sales processes, the technical product and services, and the tools and systems to support the sales. With so much information passing in front of new sales employees, absorption and comprehension would be crucial. Thus, new employees needed a comprehensive yet succinct framework that would depict how products, services, and systems fit together and affect one another.

The stakeholders determined that in order to help achieve mastery-level understanding, they needed an intensive, boot-camp-like experiential learning solution. It would need to be extremely realistic, immediately applicable to day-to-day selling activities, and, above all, it needed to improve the Speed to Performance for new sales representatives.

After completing the Simulation Decision Tree, IEC decided that a classroom-based simulation that fused product and services knowledge with a solution selling process would be their optimal solution.

Regis University
STRATEGY

ORGANIZATION HISTORY

Regis University is a Jesuit university in Denver, CO with over 15,000 students. The University is comprised of three schools: Regis College's undergraduate liberal arts school, the Rueckert-Hartman School for Health Professions, and the School for Professional Studies.

The School for Professional Studies (SPS) offers programs for adults. Today, more than 13,000 students are involved in SPS' accelerated adult education programs, which include a variety of options to accommodate students' educational goals, learning preferences and lifestyle. The School for Professional Studies offers sixteen bachelor's degrees, seven master's degrees, and over twenty advanced certificates.

CHALLENGES AND ISSUES

One of the most popular SPS programs is the Master of Business Administration (MBA). The Regis MBA program is respected in both the business and academic communities, and its on-line program draws students from around the world. But strong competition from other business schools–both in Colorado and globally–led Regis to look for ways to differentiate their program and make it more attractive both to potential students and to companies who hire MBAs.

For years, the capstone class of the Regis MBA program was a traditional case-analysis-driven program. As in countless other MBA programs across the country, students spent the semester reading case studies and writing papers on a variety of topics. There was nothing wrong with this traditional approach, but there was nothing particularly exciting about it, either.

After talking to a number of companies that hire MBA graduates, Regis realized that employers were no longer looking for students with "book knowledge." Companies wanted to hire people who knew how to run a business, not people who just knew *about* running a business.

Regis' business goal was to be the largest and most effective on-line MBA program in the nation. To accomplish this, they recognized the need to be both different and better than their competition. One of the strategies they adopted was to build a new capstone course that combined the intellectual rigor of traditional MBA classes with an experiential element that would allow students to apply what they had learned during the program.

In other words, in order to give employers graduates who knew how to run a business, Regis University wanted to give students a chance to do it.

APPLYING THE SIMULATION DECISION TREE

This was obviously a learning solution, so the first step of the Decision Tree was easy to figure out. The next step—determine the richness of the solution—was also easy with such a clear strategy: allow students to run a multi-billion dollar company by utilizing the skills learned within the MBA program and from the real world.

The students had already developed a solid foundation by nearly completing the MBA program. So the university's objective was to develop the student's skills to a mastery level so they could clearly evaluate the cause-and-effect relationship between their decisions and the outcomes of their decisions.

The third step—determining if a simulation was the right solution—took some time. To be precise, it took Regis almost two years from conception to reality. During that time Regis evaluated dozens of options. They examined on-line case studies and games, evaluated web-based courses, and tried video streaming live classes to on-line students using "webinars."

Although these solutions provided value, and the original case study method had worked for the better part of a century to prepare Regis MBA students, the university needed a learning solution that would push students to the next level of performance and better prepare them for the increasingly competitive real-life business world.

The faculty outlined their extensive expectations of the new capstone course clearly: teach students to think strategically, build critical- and systems-thinking skills, deal with multiple influencers, and work in teams to solve business problems. Clearly, a simulation was the right solution.

2.2 IMPLEMENTERS

Reflect on two or three things you've learned that you will never forget. Most likely you learned those things by practice or by trial and error. These repeatable processes etched the lesson into your memory.

Practice is a good start, but it won't help unless you also have the knowledge of what to practice. Combining practice with knowledge is what creates a great piano player—or a successful employee.

Knowledge is the internalization of information, data, and experiences. Everything a person reads, sees, hears, or does adds to his or her knowledge base. Combine knowledge with practice, and employees begin to create new meanings and ideas. They begin to advance from awareness to literacy and further.

In the first part of the SIMTEC model, we discussed the importance of identifying a strategy tied to the business goal. In order to implement a strategy, employees often need to understand various business practices and how they interrelate. A business practice, such as product development or solution selling, consists of various processes that require both knowledge and skills to implement.

Implementers define the knowledge and skills necessary to effectively perform a business practice.

How does this all come together? Imagine you're part of the executive team at a large retail store chain. Wall Street analysts are concerned that the company's mid-year revenue results may fall short of projections. You can't afford to wait and see if the results hit the targets; you need to take action *now* to address the concerns while there is still time to make a difference. Looking for a quick and practical solution, you ask the district managers and training team to define plans for improving revenue. After lengthy discussions, the team decides that improving daily gross profit is the key to increased revenue.

Your store managers point out the if the employees could more effectively implement the business practices of merchandising, inventory management, advertising, and analyzing sales data they would improve gross profit. To affect your bottom line, they don't need to do more than understand these skills on an intellectual level, though; they need to apply them on a daily basis. They need to understand how decisions about each aspect of running their stores affect other decisions. A manager cannot effectively merchandise the wrong inventory, and making the right inventory decisions depends heavily on extracting intelligence from sales data.

A traditional approach to addressing this training issue is to provide the employees with instruction in separate business practices and trust them to make the connections. For example, a merchandising workshop would provide an employee with hands-on experience on stacking and organizing products. A workbook, job-aid, and process guides could instruct employees on the appropriate way to manage inventory. An e-learning course on advertising would provide the employees with the essential knowledge of basic advertising techniques and concepts. Finally, a workbook with example reports would point out which key data items to watch and how to perform basic calculations.

This example solution, which is a very typical blended approach, provides the essential foundational knowledge but fails to demonstrate how

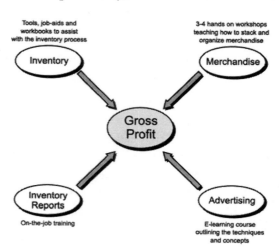

Typical Training Solution

the various business practices interrelate to improve gross profit.

How could a simulation help the retail chain implement this strategy? Instead of hearing about the importance of inventory or understanding the basic principles of merchandising (applying the intelligence in the sales data), store managers immersed in a simulation receive hands-on experience trying to improve gross profit. Learners employ various aspects of all four Implementers. While doing so, they are able to see how their decisions regarding inventory and merchandising and their interpretation of sales data impact gross profit–and ultimately their own bonus! They learn from their own successes and from their failures, seeing the big picture and how the various areas of the business interrelate. They gain confidence.

Why are Implementers important? Take a look at the following diagram:

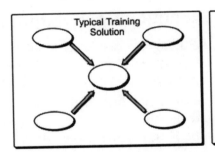 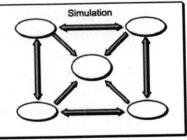

A simulation provides an environment where an employee can learn the cause-and-effect relationship of the Implementers without real-world consequences. Implementers are important because they drive design of the simulation and provide the justification for a simulation business case.

In the next section, you'll learn how to create a simple Execution Case Diagram. These diagrams serve as the roadmap for creating the simulation model and identifying the content needed to create a realistic and relevant simulation.

Does this mean that e-learning, lectures, and other learning solutions are not needed? Not at all! A simulation is best used when existing learning solutions are leveraged, creating a Speed to Performance™ environment for employees to practice, evaluate, and refine their skills.

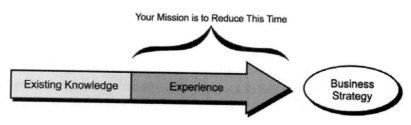

When you look at all the Implementers and consider the desired performance levels for certain business needs, traditional learning solutions are obviously not enough. They only provide one part of what is needed—the knowledge. Simulations provide the second part—the confidence to do it!

Creating a Simple Execution Case Diagram

An *Execution Case Diagram* serves as a simple yet highly effective way to visualize which Implementers to include in a simulation.

When creating a simulation, the first step is to develop a model (the brains behind the simulation) that captures the important aspects of the business necessary to implement the strategy—and no more than that. Complicated models can be too expensive to develop, too difficult to explain, and take a long time for the employees to understand. On the other end of the scale, models that are too simple might not engage or challenge the employee to develop new skills.

To begin, write your business strategy and draw a circle around it. Then identify the key business practices that an employee should be able to perform effectively in order to implement the strategy. Don't try to limit the number of practices as this point.

Recall the case of the retail chain that needs to increase gross profit by training store managers to apply knowledge and skills from merchandising, inventory management, advertising, and sales data analysis. In that case, merchandising encompasses many skills, such as knowing where to place products, how to partner products for cross-selling, how to catch a consumer's eye using price downs, and how to determine high gross profit items.

Once you've created an the first level of the ECD, you now need to identify what are the most important things employee need to know and be able to do in a particular business practice. As you go through this process, consider the following four questions:

1) What things in the business practice are the hardest for people to learn in a classroom setting? For example, are there skills that can only be built through practice or experience?

2) What key aspects of the business should the employees understand in the training? Consider people who are fully expert in this area. What do they know that makes them more valuable than the others? For the target audience of the training, what are the top mistakes they make? The model should demonstrate as many of these elements as possible—the right things as well as the mistakes.

3) What are the important measurements of the relevant parts of the business? If effective inventory management is one of the important business

practices, what are the standard measures that managers are evaluated on in your business, and what do the best managers look at in monitoring and managing different inventory situations? The important measures should be included in the model.

4) What are the important aspects of the business that the student can control? For example, can they change stocking levels of different parts, and is that important to the goals of the training? Can they add or remove staff, and is that important? Can they change order and size of orders, and is that important? All of the important controls should be included in the model.

To help remember these questions think about What, Where, and How:

- What do the experts do?
- Where do they look for information?
- How do they do it?

The answers to these questions will help you identify the primary Implementers and provide the overall definition to create the simulation model and business case. The connecting lines between the implementer are used to define their relationships to one another.

A more complicated ECD diagram includes Implementation Profiles that define:

- The decisions and actions that employees need to make within the simulation
- The data and reports that needed to make the decisions or perform the actions

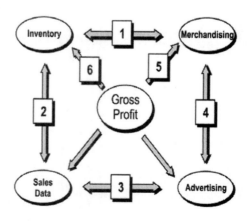

- The measurements and conditions to evaluate the decisions and actions
- The causes-and-effects that a decision or action may have on another decision or action

For the scope of this book however, a simple ECD will be enough to understand the SIMTEC model and gain executive support.

Why is a simple ECD important to executives?

Executives looking at the diagram can see their own thinking depicted in the ECD. Many business strategies require employees to effectively and efficiently perform various business practices. The diagram illustrates that the interdependencies between the various business practices is critical to achieving the business strategy. Executives fully understand for the power of an employee grasping the impact that slight modifications to decisions and actions may have on a business strategy. However, executives also know that this level of understanding takes years of experience. A well-designed simulation could potentially decrease the time it takes to develop this understanding and therefore make the employees more productive faster.

International Electronics Company
IMPLEMENTERS

SOLUTION OVERVIEW

IEC's learning group needed to implement a solution that would achieve their strategic goal while containing the training costs involved. They also needed to limit the amount of time new sales employees had to be "off the floor" and away from their jobs. Finally, the learning group needed a solution that would address not only the technical product and services skills covered in the old program, but also of the recently-prioritized solution selling process.

73

IEC already offered workshops, videos, manuals, and other resources on the electronic products and services they carried, but they needed to identify a new method for sales representatives to master *selling* in order to align with the new "Total Value Selling" approach. In other words, IEC needed to give their employees an environment in which to practice the processes and skills that would move them from "order-taking" to "value-selling."

IEC's internal stakeholders gathered to participate in a "design day," where they explored how to address their identified business goals and mapped out a solution. When they emerged from a conference room eight hours later, they had confirmed the strategic goal, defined their strategies, and documented the Implementers. IEC decided that in order to implement the strategy, their salespeople needed to be able to identify customer needs, determine appropriate products and services to meet customer needs, and focus on "value selling" instead of order taking.

With these implementers in mind, IEC was ready to move forward designing the simulation.

Regis University
IMPLEMENTERS

SOLUTION OVERVIEW

Once Regis University staff decided that a simulation was the best solution for their business need, they decided to design a simulation that challenged students to apply all of the skills they acquired during the MBA program. They needed to ensure that students in a Denver classroom and students accessing remotely from anywhere in the world could use the simulation equally well. In short, Regis needed a solution that allowed both classroom and on-line students to experience running a real company, to make decisions in all functional areas, to work in teams, evaluate their impact, and refine their decisions and actions—and it needed to feel real.

Based on the Speed to Performance model, the students already had an existing knowledge base of the main functional areas of business: Sales, Marketing, Finance, Operations, and Human Resources. Regis decided to implement a simulation that would allow students to quickly apply this knowledge to running a business. This decision supported the business goal of becoming the largest on-line MBA program in the nation in two ways: 1) Corporations seeking students with experiential learning experiences would favor hiring Regis MBA graduates because of the practical nature of the training, and 2) Students would be attracted to Regis' MBA program because they know that it offers a firm knowledge base and a valuable experiential learning component.

Based on their analysis of their business goal, their challenges, and their strategy, decided to implement a complex simulation that put teams of students in charge of daily operations of a fictional, multi-billion-dollar, transnational athletic shoe company.

2.3 MOTIVATORS

Countless reams of paper have been used to print the vast number of research papers, books, theories, models, and tools that attempt to explain motivation. You would think that with all this research we would have some answers, but unfortunately that isn't the case. Depending on what you read, you'll learn that higher pay motivates employees, or that it doesn't; internal motivation is the key, or external motivation is all that matters.

Yet one thing we do know is that motivation is critical to learning. Successful execution of a strategy requires engaged employees who are committed to the success of the organization and are motivated to perform well.[16]

Frederick Herzberg has focused his research on what motivates employees in the workplace, with three interesting results. First, certain conditions in the workplace dampen motivation: poor training, mindless bureaucracy, bad supervision, substandard pay, uncooperative teammates, and unsafe conditions. Conversely, his second finding says that removing these negatives will not result in increased employee motivation.

Motivation, by definition, lies within the individual. Herzberg determined that external influences, such as promised rewards and threatened sanctions, have temporary and limited impact on behavior or performance.

Herzberg concludes that employees are motivated by the opportunity to grow, to develop, to contribute, to learn, and to otherwise find meaning in their efforts at work.[17]

Few companies realize this ideal. In eye-opening research published in the *Wall Street Journal*, Gallup found that nineteen percent of the 1,000 people it interviewed were "actively disengaged" at work. These workers complained that they didn't have the tools they needed to do their jobs. The poll also indicated that employees didn't know what was expected of them, and they felt they didn't have the adequate skills to achieve performance at the levels necessary for success.[18]

The same Gallup results found that only a third of employees were "fully engaged," and the remaining half (48%) were "not engaged." Two out of three employees surveyed in typical workplaces were not motivated to perform well!

Simulations are one way to increase employee motivation, allowing them to engage fully in the various aspects of the company and emotionally invest in its success. Thinking about your participants' motivation as you design your simulation will help you:

- Address what motivates employees before, during, and after the simulation. This can be achieved by creating Implementer requirements for each time period.
- Set clear expectations. This can be accomplished by defining goals and milestones which participants need to achieve.
- Hold participants accountable. This can be accomplished by creating team tasks and integrating teambuilding components.
- Ensure that the simulation allows for both success and failure. This can be accomplished by tweaking the emotional throttle, which is further explained in the following pages.
- Leverage participants' natural competitive tendencies. Even when the simulation design de-emphasizes competition, participants naturally want to win. They strive to surpass one another, or to improve their performance against the simulation itself. This can be accomplished by publishing selected team results, having the teams select goals or make a presentation to the other teams, have an open group discussion or de-brief after the completion of each round.

> One widely accepted theory of adult motivation, called expectancy theory, holds that when faced with a new experience or challenge adults ask themselves three questions:
>
> *If I take the risks involved in doing this new task, am I likely to succeed?*
>
> *If I succeed, will there be a reward for my efforts?*
>
> *Does the reward make the effort worthwhile?*
>
> People asked to participate in a learning simulation in the workplace will surely consider these three questions.

Ultimately, a simulation is about producing results. Keep this in mind, because the simulation will be one of the most challenging training programs your employees will go through. It will also likely be their most rewarding and memorable experience.

Know Your Participants

Before you try to apply specific motivation techniques to a simulation, be sure you know your participants. Gathering participant requirements at the beginning will help you understand what motivates them and what may discourage, distress, or even disengage them. This is critical to the engagement and effectiveness of the simulation. That is why motivation, as the SIMTEC model illustrates, wraps around the Implementers and threads through the technology and tools, environment, and content dimensions.

Here are some questions for you to consider when you're putting together your motivation requirements.

Dimensions	Do the participants ...
Technology and Tools	▪ Understand computers and how to use them well (computer savvy), or are they mostly beginners? ▪ Use the Internet regularly and feel comfortable with browser software?
Environment	▪ Thrive on competition, or do they avoid it? ▪ Work independently or prefer teams? ▪ Prefer many fast-paced rounds or fewer rounds with more time? ▪ Require many debriefing and feedback opportunities or just a few?
Content	▪ Prefer a lot of details or the big picture? ▪ Prefer spreadsheets, visual charts, or both? ▪ Require a lot of reference materials or just simple reminders? ▪ Prefer a lot of feedback in different forms or just a few bullet points? ▪ Prefer lots of graphics and video or simple diagrams and text?

Prepare the Participants

When you hear the word "simulation," what first comes to mind? If you were told that you'll be going through a simulation in which you'll be running a portion of your company's business and that you're expected to achieve certain goals, what do you think? In general, people think that simulations are great tools. However, given the demands that simulations typically place on learners, some employees are apprehensive, especially at the outset.

Often, first-time participants have many different questions when they first approach a simulation. Will the experience make me look dumb in front of my peers? My manager? What will I learn about myself? Can I do it? Depending on the person, these fears can inhibit a participant to the point that she can't learn.

Why this love-hate relationship? It's hard to argue with the fact that most simulations are highly engaging and that most adults learn best through experience–and a simulation, at its core, is an experiential tool. On the other hand, experience is often associated with failure. We learn great lessons by trying, failing, and then trying again.

Too little tension creates boredom or indifference; too much tension brings feelings of anxiety, fear of failure, and embarrassment. Just enough fosters learning.

In simulations, fear of failure often leads to employee apprehension. Sometimes apprehension evolves into a problematic reaction like withdrawal, anger, or defensiveness. Learners are not accustomed to failing in training situations, because most traditional programs provide so little tension that concepts like failure, accountability, expectations, and results rarely come into play.

In fact, one of the reasons that traditional programs often fail to make lasting impressions on employees is that they do not incorporate these areas of significant tension, which we have seen are vital to the retention of knowledge. Remember, simulations provide a safe environment. Learners can make mistakes without the business suffering the consequences. Therefore, encourage learners to take risks and create an atmosphere that encourages them to openly disclose their concerns, problems, and anxiety during workplace simulations. Usually, when people make mistakes they feel guilty and embarrassed, and they try to hide or minimize their failure. When that happens, the opportunity to learn from the mistake is hidden, as well. In a well-built simulation environment, mistakes are simply part of the learning and growth.

Employee learners are likely to have a number of questions as they begin a simulation experience. The way in which these questions are answered dramatically impacts motivation, engagement, and learning during the simulation.

People want to know if the simulation will:

- Let me know what is expected of me?
- Help me understand how I impact the business?
- Improve my skills?
- Advance my skills and knowledge in fields related to my job?
- Perform better in my current job in the eyes of my managers?
- Help me attain better pay or a promotion?
- Prepare me for my next job search?

The emotional throttle

Emotion affects everything we learn. Adults learn most and best when they feel a passion for learning and the learning process. Without that emotional engagement, new lessons fade from memory quickly; when associated with strong emotions, however, new lessons become ingrained and eventually integrated into performance.

This doesn't necessarily mean that one's passion for a subject needs to be positive in order for true learning to take place. Consider, for example, a man who became familiar with the work of William Faulkner several years ago; to this day, he despises Faulkner's writing. If you ask him why, you're apt to get an earful about *exactly* why he doesn't like Faulkner, complete with references to specific works and examples of the author's style. This is a great example of how emotion—be it positive, negative, or somewhere in-between—helps to anchor knowledge in our minds. Despite his negative emotions associate with Faulkner's work, the man in question still retained the information. If he had been uninterested in or disconnected from the writings (i.e., if he hadn't hated them so much!), he wouldn't have remembered much about Faulkner, much less specific details about his work.

Researchers have long documented the connection between emotional engagement, memory, and learning. According to Steven Johnson in his book *Mind Wide Open*, emotional engagement related to learning is so powerful that it possesses the potential to "alter memory organization so that cognitive material is better integrated and diverse ideas are seen as more related."[19] Advances in brain science over the past twenty-five years have documented how this emotional anchoring of experience in our memories occurs on chemical and electrical cellular levels in the brain.

A good business simulation draws users emotionally into a virtual environment that parallels the real world. Instead of merely directing learners to read about business ethics, for example, simulations ask employees to actually take the responsibilities and deal with the ethical dilemmas and crises of conscience that they would in real life.

In a simulation, learning and doing happen simultaneously. For instance, how do managers resolve conflicts between the best interests of their employees and customers and the bottom line? Should they choose the short-term benefit to the company or long-term health and viability? What weight should the company's role as neighbor in the community or citizen of the country play in the decision? In a simulation, such ethical dilemmas are not merely hypothetical. Instead, learners wrestle with conflicting rights and wrongs. In the process, they almost inevitably develop a strong emotional reaction to the struggle, just as they would in the real world.

Other design elements—from gaming and collaboration to acceleration and exploration—also contribute to the emotional richness of a simulated experience. As participants contend with their simulation team members, for example, emotions run high and conflict inevitably occurs. As learners anxiously await feedback about their success in a particular round, self-doubt, anxiety, fear, apprehension, and finally the agony of failure or the joy of success percolate within each of them.

Sometimes, a high-impact simulation evokes emotions that participants handle internally, never openly disclosing or discussing their feelings. These emotions may be directed at themselves, specific events that occur within the simulation, or at the simulation as a whole.

This range of emotions changes throughout most simulations. In the beginning, for example, employees often tend to feel a certain degree of hesitancy and nervousness simply because they aren't sure what to expect. After this initial trepidation passes and they begin to immerse themselves in the obstacles and challenges of the simulated environment wholeheartedly, participants begin to feel a variety of other emotions, from frustration and anger to elation and excitement.

These emotional experiences can have lasting effects on decision-makers for years to come, because the emotions experienced within a simulation help to ingrain the experiences in learners' minds. Days, weeks, months, and even years later, when that employee encounters a real-world situation similar to what he experienced in the simulation, the same emotional responses will flood back to him, bringing with them memories and lessons learned.

Lesson Learned: Emotional Throttle

Amid all of the turmoil and chaos of our hectic lives, we constantly filter various inputs and react to situations the best ways we can. The speed at which we often have to fast-paced and important decisions adds tension to our lives in the real world -- and explains why tension is a key part of effective, high-impact simulations.

The key to creating an effective simulation is optimizing the balance by creating an environment that feels like the real world, but not so much that participants are too anxious or afraid to take risks, make mistakes, and explore alternatives.

The information you gather about participants and what motivates them will help you make effective content, framework, and technology design decisions—which, in turn, will adjust the simulation's emotional throttle appropriately.

For example, when making content decisions for a simulation, you will need to determine the size and scope of supporting materials provided to participants before, during, and after the simulation. Too little information before the simulation might make participants nervous and anxious. Too much information, however, might detract from the "realness" of the simulation or overwhelm the learners with data. (After all, how many times have you taken over a new role or launched a new product and had someone give you all the details up front?)

Define Goals and Milestones

An effective simulation, like any other worthwhile corporate learning solution, needs a clearly-defined goal. Goals give participants something to work toward and supply a sense of satisfaction when they are achieved.

There are two types of goals that can be attached to a simulation. The first is a big picture, global goal for the simulation as a whole. This broad goal usually is one that the participant either achieves or fails to achieve by the end of the simulation.

An example of this kind of global goal would be, "This business has been losing money. Turn it around and make it successful, make your stock rise, and expand your business so that it becomes a multinational company." An overall goal such as this should sit in the back of learners' minds at all times during the simulation so that they don't get lost in the details of day-to-day issues.

The second level of simulation goals focuses on interim checkpoints (also called mini-goals). When reached, these checkpoints let the employee know that she is on the right path to achieving the overall goal of the simulation. If the leaner fails to reach her checkpoints, chances are she will not obtain her overall goal either unless she changes something. Often, strong emotions and key learning occurs following feedback at checkpoints during a simulation.

In a simulation, checkpoint goals might be, "Within the next fiscal year, make your company's stock rise four points, increase productivity by ten percent, expand your workforce by less than five percent, and achieve profitability." Such mini-goals provide learners a sense of satisfaction when they are reached. This is especially important within simulations, where emotions and frustrations often play such a prominent role. Achieving mini-goals also helps boost learners' confidence and gives them the courage they need to try different strategies and tactics.

If learners fail to achieve their mini-goals, simulation facilitators often interpret this as a sign that the participants need additional feedback to focus their efforts on improving performance before they reach the next checkpoint.

Lesson Learned: Simulations and Personal Goals

Just as in real life, goals embedded within a simulation give employees a direction to work toward.

A high-impact business simulation must have clearly defined goals for the simulation as a whole (extrinsic goals). This is a target that employees attempt to obtain or exceed, such as a sales target, a certain percentage of market share, or a safety rating.

Learners' personal intrinsic goals cannot be supplied by the simulation, but they are present nevertheless and affect every action. This is because intrinsic goals are fused into individual identities. For example, an employee's intrinsic goals might include climbing the corporate ladder as quickly as possible, being a good husband or wife, or helping others as much as possible. Each of these things will affect the way the individual thinks and acts both in real life and in the simulation.

Many of the more sophisticated business simulations allow employees to not only define, but also to track, their progress toward meeting extrinsic goals. Personal, intrinsic goals, of course, cannot be tracked. There is no "pass" or "fail" grade given for this type of learning within a simulation. However, there is a way to determine whether employees achieved their intrinsic goals. At the beginning of the simulation, have each person write down two or three personal goals. When the simulation ends, ask if they achieved their goals.

Create Teamwork and Team-building Opportunities

To enhance learning, you can opt to create teams. Participants broken into groups will collaborate with each other while proceeding through the simulation.

Collaboration is conducive to learning for many reasons. Sometimes a team creates a supportive environment in which learners can contend with their emotions together. When participants are first introduced to simulation learning, for example, they often are intimidated and respond tentatively to initial tasks and decisions. Why? Because at first glance, a simulation represents a departure from the familiar; it differs greatly from the traditional training to which so many of us are accustomed.

Working collaboratively within a team, however, can help put individual employees at ease, lowering their stress levels. Placed in a foreign environment, team members quickly realize that they are not alone in experiencing uncertainty and anxiety. While working collaboratively within a simulation, learners often begin to rely on one another for support and for mutual commiseration, ultimately leading to stronger teams and, as a result, more effective communication and collaboration.

This shared experience factor in learning is a powerful learning tool. People who have played on championship athletic teams, survived combat with a squad of soldiers, or worked as members of a highly-functioning surgical, sales, or management team often vividly remember these times as peak experiences because of the people around them.

Team-building, in fact, is the second reason why collaboration is conducive to the learning process and to managing the emotional throttle. Even after learners' initial fears are put to rest, teams continue to bond over time because of the inherently emotional nature of simulations.

Sometimes teams fail to collaborate, which they quickly discover is a plan to fail, a valuable lesson itself. Simulation participants learn that a team is more than a collection of individuals or experts. When a group has not yet formed itself into a team (and there is a difference!), it is common for them to split work evenly. Each member does his or her assignment, often without contact with other group members. In this situation, groups can essentially be reduced to individually-excellent performances that collectively fail.

However, groups immersed in a simulation quickly discover that simply splitting up the work is not effective. If each individual is assigned a different aspect of the business to manage, she or he will make decisions that are best for that part of the company. The simulation quickly shows that those choices might not be best for the whole business. Indeed, in simulations individual experts who know and independently take the "best" course of action in their individual areas of expertise and responsibility are unpleasantly surprised when the collective result is lacking because of actions taken in their particular area.

Because the different parts of a simulation affect one another, participants soon learn that effective communication among the various departments and dimensions of the organization must exist at all times, or the company will fail.

For example, in reviewing his department's goals and objectives, one team member might decide that budget cuts need to be made and that personnel need to be eliminated.

Without communicating this plan to team members in other departments, he decides to lay off ten people.

Meanwhile, and also unbeknownst to the others, another team member in another department is attempting to expand one of the company's product lines—a move that will require the organization to hire additional personnel. Had both team members communicated their decisions to each other beforehand, there would have been less needless hiring and firing—saving the organization time and money.

When implementing a simulation that calls for collaboration, think carefully when assigning participants to each team. To get the best cross-learning results, teams should be as diverse as possible. If possible, don't create a team only comprised of engineers, accountants, marketers, or salespeople; blend backgrounds.

Creating diverse simulation teams has two benefits. First, it gives each team a broader base of knowledge, allowing them to perform more effectively within the simulation. In addition, once employees return to the real world, cross-departmental communication within the company is likely to improve. When people from different departments work together in a simulation, they form a relationship that inevitably extends to their day-to-day jobs.

With that understood, many simulations will include only a single group of participants or job roles, such as a sales simulation designed solely for sales representatives or an engineering simulation designed solely for engineers. In these instances, creating multifunctional teams is obviously not a possibility. That's all right. You still can form exceptionally diverse teams by considering elements such as job history, education, personal and professional background, and personality when selecting members for each team.

Team exercises allow employees to experience and understand different reactions that others have to the same or similar events. Simulation teams also allow participants to understand and appreciate the different skills that their teammates possess, opening up lines of communication that may not have previously existed. When Jim from accounting goes to the sales department after the simulation, he will know to look for Mike (with whom he worked in a team-based customer-service simulation a month before). He also will know far more about Mike's capabilities and feel confident that Mike will be able to help him, because Mike solved a similar problem within the simulation.

Despite the common "wisdoms" that putting the nose to the grindstone with minimal distractions is the only way to be efficient and remain focused on the task at hand, simulations teach that working in a vacuum has its drawbacks. A worker or department that fails to interact and communicate effectively with others runs the risk of duplicating work unnecessarily, thereby missing important opportunities, making poor or uninformed business decisions, and wasting time and money.

Indeed, performance experts report that a common reason for organizational performance problems is the failure to communicate key information to the right people in the right place at the right time.

Lesson Learned: Collaboration and Cooperation

According to Carl Larson—author of *When Teams Work Best: 6,000 Team Members and Leaders Tell What It Takes to Succeed and Teamwork: What Must Go Right/What Can Go Wrong* —cooperative learning is one of the most effective tools for accelerating Speed to Performance. When employees work together in teams, says Larson, they learn more and they learn it more quickly than they ever would if they were working alone.

In addition to giving employees the opportunity to discuss questions and problems, collaboration also affords participants the benefits associated with hearing others' perspectives and developing important interpersonal communication skills.

Most of the better business simulations include elements of collaboration and teamwork. Even if a simulation design calls for employees to work primarily on their own, there should still be opportunities for collaboration in discussion groups or debriefs. The class as a whole should be invited to ask questions and discuss the answers. Ideally, when the content and motivators align well with teamwork, simulations should require teamwork for success.

Collaboration positively impacts learners' levels of motivation. Athletes train more effectively with another person than they do alone. They push and challenge each other on a daily basis, ultimately enabling each athlete to better individual performance. Similarly, individuals working alone in the workplace can easily get bogged down or even lose their sense of motivation. Working as a group, however, provides an opportunity for employees to push one another through such situations.

Researchers Johnson, Maruyama, Johnson, Nelson, and Skon concluded that "There is considerable evidence indicating that students working cooperatively perform better than do students working individually."[20] This is partially because of the motivation factor and partially because of *cross learning*.

Cross learning occurs when each individual on a team has a different background and life experiences. Members with varied knowledge pools help "fill in the gaps" of knowledge, allowing the team as a whole to become more effective. If a question comes up, the chances that someone in the group will already possess the necessary information increase significantly as the group size increases.

Learning in teams through simulations ultimately teaches the invaluable lesson that a group of people is always smarter than any one of them working alone.

International Electronics Company
MOTIVATORS

IEC's new sales employees came from a wide variety of backgrounds. Some had years of sales experience, while others had almost none. To meet the needs of all employees, IEC's new simulation needed to be challenging enough to hook those with more experience while teaching them the unique approach to the company's product and selling process, but it also had to provide an easy-to-understand, easy-to-apply selling foundation for those who had less sales experience.

The simulation also needed to attract participants' attention, motivate new representatives to participate (by making the simulation as relevant to their jobs as possible), and evoke emotions that would keep employees engaged for the entire program. An experience this powerful would create a lasting impact that could significantly improve a new sales employee's performance.

IEC hired an outside training company to provide a custom simulation put new sales representatives into situations identical to those in their real-world business environment. The BRIDGE™ Solution Selling Process focused on specific sales skills woven into a four-day, in-house technical product and service training. The simulation provided a competitive, team-based program that involved multiple customer calls and culminated with final sales presentations to a client "decision board."

At the end of the simulation, new employees walked away with more than integrated product, service, and selling skills; they also took rich experiences that prepared them to handle situations they would surely encounter back on the job.

One of the hardest parts of introducing any new learning solution is cultivating initial interest and excitement. IEC addressed this challenge by creating a communication/roll-out plan to introduce the simulation. Initial messages clarified expectations and helped develop positive attitudes toward the sales simulation. New employees received informational messages and instructions, while separate communications to managers discussed the intended outcomes of the training and outlined their responsibilities to reinforce the lessons after the simulation.

To further increase employee motivation, IEC focused its communication on demonstrating the relevance of the training to learners' jobs, and emphasizing that the new program would build participants' confidence by enabling them to succeed both in training and on the job.

SETTING GOALS

The specific goals of IEC's training program were similar to the strategic goals determined at the beginning of the process. After a new hire completed the simulation, she was expected to know how to:

Understand IEC's products and services and know how to use them to address customer needs.

Use IEC's unique selling approach to save customers' time and deliver the right products and services for their needs.

Understand how to use the unique sales approach in a wide variety of customer situations.

Listen to customer needs and ask the right questions to find out what the real issues are.

TEAMWORK AND TEAM BUILDING

In IEC's version of the BRIDGE™ sales simulation, teamwork was crucial to the learning solution. From the beginning, teams knew that they were competing with each other for business. On the first day of the four-day simulation, the facilitator assigned participants to teams. Each team was required to work together to research the prospective client organization, prepare for and conduct sales calls, interview customers, and complete call follow-up activities.

In order to ensure that each team member participated fully in the simulation, each customer call was led by a different person on each team. After each call, the lead salesperson received feedback based on specific selling competencies. During the next call, a different member of the team became the lead salesperson, and the process continued. Since every member of the team knew that they would eventually lead the team, individual learners were eager to work together and make each call successful.

Throughout the simulation, participants received feedback in several ways, including customer debriefings, individual team meetings, and facilitated discussions with all of the teams together. Various competency-based forms provided the structure needed to quickly capture both the quantitative and qualitative feedback for each team and team member.

Regis University
MOTIVATORS

Motivating MBA students to participate in their simulation was a challenge for the Regis University staff.

Initially, Regis' MBA faculty believed that students would be excited to change the pace of the program and compete in an on-line simulation. For the most part, they found the opposite to be true. Students worried that the simulation would identify their weaknesses or destroy their perfect grade-point averages, worried they would not be able to figure out how to run the multi-billion dollar business, and the list went on.

The failure of the initial round of the university capstone course was a perfect example of what can happen when decision-makers overlook critical steps of the SIMTEC model. In this case, Regis made incorrect assumptions about students' initial motivations, underestimated the impact of their negative emotions and fears, and didn't adequately motivate the students before the simulation began.

To improve the simulation, RLS went back to the model and reviewed all the top design elements: Pre-Simulation Objectives, Setting Goals, Working in Teams, and Managing the Emotional Throttle.

PRE-SIMULATION OBJECTIVES

The first few groups of students went into the simulation without information about the experience, the objectives of the simulation, or what would be expected of them. On top of that, they were not sure how their performance would be evaluated and how it would affect their grades. For the typically results-driven, highly competitive MBA student, earning an A was paramount.

To address this issue, RLS created a simulation Welcome Package. It contained a Mercury Shoes commercial, testimonials and helpful hints from students and professors, a Mercury shoes annual report, market analysis report, product and service descriptions, and three years of historical financial data for the fictional company. Regis University's dean provided incoming students with clear objectives and expectations.

These proactive steps seemed to lessen Regis students' fears to essential nervousness.

SETTING GOALS

As the simulation rounds progressed, students' motivational levels deteriorated. The simulation lacked clearly defined goals and milestones. As a result, students were frustrated because they did not know if they were succeeding. To address this issue, the following goals and milestones where created:

Performance Indexes–a series of key indicators were generated and presented each round. These indexes provided students a single-number overall evaluation of how they and their teammates performed.

Trends Reports–various reports compared actual results and forecasted results to help students think through setting future-oriented targets.

Management Reports–various management reports from each business unit provided students with a snapshot and historical information of the impact their decisions were having in individual areas.

Faculty Evaluations–faculty members established deadlines, to the day and hour, for teams to complete tasks for each round. When students "closed the books" and submitted their final decisions for a particular round, faculty reviewed the team's inputs and offered Socratic–style questions and ideas using an on-line bulletin board.

Team Debriefs–debriefs mostly helped to unify the teams. The objective was to get teams to discuss openly their successes and missteps, and to evaluate their companies' performances. In doing so, they would discover their dependencies and serve as coaches to each other. The result was a more confident team.

CREATING TEAMWORK AND TEAMBUILDING OPPORTUNITIES

Teamwork was not a problem in the simulation. In order for the students to accomplish all the tasks provided, they had to work in teams.

Teambuilding, however, proved to be a serious issue for some teams. Since students were located all over the country and could not meet in person, it required creativity to get them to work together.

A few times, students requested to "fire" other members of their teams. One enlightening instance occurred when a single individual asked for permission to fire his *entire* team. The faculty member wisely counseled him to try to work with the others to resolve issues and problems. At the end of the week, when the team completed their tasks and "closed the books," a turn of events occurred. The individual who wanted to fire the rest of the team had made seriously bad decisions—mainly because he elected not to work with the others on his team. As a result, the team asked for permission to fire the individual. Now that's humbling!

The simulation modeled the real world so well that faculty reported being able to identify which teams would fail and which would succeed by watching how well they worked together as a team.

Regis University developed a variety of solutions to address the teamwork and teambuilding elements. They established conference calls, on-line discussion groups, and general guidelines. However, the best solution came in the reminders from faculty that "In the real world you do not always get a chance to select your team or switch members when you feel like it, so figure it out."

EMOTIONAL THROTTLE

Just like in the real world, many factors contribute to making a simulation stressful. Some stressors were intentionally designed into the simulation, and others evolved as students ran their business. The Regis University team took about six months of constant adjusting to find the right balance.

The first emotional issue related to the Pre-Simulation objectives. The students wanted everything clearly laid out. What is the goal? How much money should we make in this division? What is the right amount of inventory to carry? What percentage of market share should we shoot for in Europe? How much money should we spend in marketing? Exactly what do you want my role to be and how should I do it?

To create a manageable environment as close as possible to the real world, the Regis faculty and RLS staff settled on the following:

1) Faculty assigned teams to create a mix of skill areas, but it was up to team members to further identify strengths and weaknesses.

2) Teams needed to organize themselves into the structure they thought would best serve the business (i.e. hierarchy by function, managers of product lines, managers of regions).

3) Typical information that would be available in any company would be given to the students (company overview and history, financial and management reports, product and service descriptions, and various market and industry analysis). Additionally, various hints and instructions were added to the many tasks that students needed to complete each week. However, over time clues were reduced or removed, because the students were given too much data and were no longer challenged to think.

2.4 TECHNOLOGY AND TOOLS

No matter what kind of simulation you're building or buying, you will need tools or engines that evaluate participants' inputs and determine the impact their decisions have on the simulated business.

This underlying technology often is the most expensive and complex part of the simulation, so it's important to select what will best meet your needs. Good technology will accelerate and improve the participants' performance while making the simulation seem more realistic and authentic.

In this book, *technology* refers to any software or hardware used to evaluate decisions and track participant performance. A *tool* is a paper-based (or non-technical device) used to evaluate decisions and track participant performance. Some simulations only use technology, some use only tools, and most use a blend of both. This section focuses mainly on technology and blended solutions, because those tend to be more complex.

Understand the Technology Behind the Scene

Technologies have three main components: a *model* that performs calculations, an *input* interface that receives data supplied to the model, and an *output* interface that presents data generated by the model.

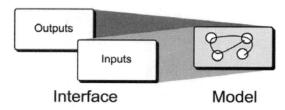

Interface   Model

Models

A *model* is a behind-the-scenes tool that represents relationships among the various functional areas or processes of a business. Models calculate the impacts that participants directly make in certain areas, as well as the indirect effects that may ripple out to other areas.

Simulation models typically contain a number of powerful engines that express various business operations. A group of connected business operations is called a *business process*. Business models integrate a number of processes.

As in any system, the model responds to direct and indirect inputs. *Direct inputs* are initiated by the participants and have an immediate impact on a specific business operation. *Indirect inputs* occur as a result of change in another part of the model, which may be caused by a participant or by an external event. Inputs can cause immediate or delayed effects in any part of the model, adding significant real-world complexity to a simulation. The cumulative effect of the interactions, the delayed effects, and the feedback loops that models make possible create a simulation that feels real, allowing students to truly experience what it's like to run a business.

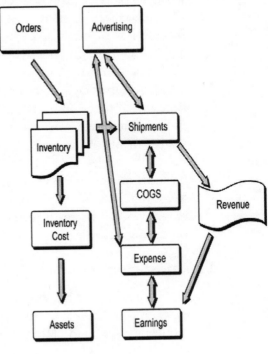

At the top (beginning) of the diagramed model, for example, simulation participants make and enter two decisions—one regarding orders for new inventory and the other regarding advertising investments.

Within the model, orders will affect inventory, inventory costs, and asset levels. Too many orders will raise inventory levels and result in reduced return on assets. Not enough orders will result in a lack of available inventory for shipments, and a failure to deliver products that could have been sold. This also creates a waste of advertising dollars, because the company won sales through ads that it could not fulfill with inventory. The business model follows and tracks each chain of effect.

Advertising decisions will affect shipments in a non-linear, indirect fashion. Beyond a certain point, increases in advertising have no effect on sales. This relationship is built into the model.

From these two decisions, the model calculates inventory levels, shipments, expenses, revenue, earnings, and asset levels. The automated system uses this information to produce income statements, balance sheets, statements of cash flows, and other specific management reports that participants expect a company to have. For each time period of the simulation, participants provide updated inputs for the two decisions (orders and advertising), and the model, in turn, provides updated versions of the financial statements and management reports.

The model depicted is much simpler than a typical business model, as it only depicts the results of two decisions. Yet even in this simple model, it is possible to see how employees can begin to foresee the impact of their decisions on the business.

The most common models

The following are the most common types of simulation evaluation models. There are many derivatives of each modeling type, and different vendors may assign different names to each model, so focus on the *characteristics* of each model when choosing a simulation.

Spreadsheet Models are the most common technologies used to create simulations, because they're easy to implement and offer a great deal of calculation power. Spreadsheets perform well when modeling linear systems, like financial simulations, but are poor at modeling complex systems. Training providers find them to be a cost-effective solution for building smaller simulations that allow employees to practice and evaluate simple business concepts.

Spreadsheets most often fall into a category called discrete simulation models. *Discrete* simulations involve individual actions that are not connected; each segment is simply a single event in time or a series of isolated events. For example, changing one value within a spreadsheet will create tangible changes on the rest of the sheet, but using spreadsheet calculations to display complex system changes (various interdependent relationships that evolve from internal and external inputs) is much more complicated. Even if it could be done, maintaining it and expanding would not be feasible.

It's worth mentioning again that spreadsheets are great for creating mini-simulations. For example, a series of mini-simulations that focuses on various skills and concepts will adequately demonstrate increasing gross profit. If the mini-simulations are packaged with the right content, they may better fit both the business needs and the budget.

Decision Tree Engines are simple branching logic trees similar to the *Choose Your Own Adventure* children's books. If the participant chooses one action, he will be sent down a pre-determined path. If he chooses another, he will be sent down another path, and so on. Because of the pre-determined nature of these

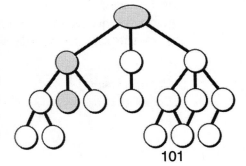

engines, they typically are best suited for simulations that focus on working step-by-step through a problem.

A decision tree engine is perfect for learners who need to acquire a skill that requires a great deal of repetition and has a known set of possible outcomes. Evaluating performance is a relatively easy task with a simple decision engine simulation, because each choice can be labeled as "Best," "Okay," or "Inadequate." The computer can assign scores to the different labels and determine how an employee did overall.

To illustrate, examine the tree diagram to the right. The top node symbolizes a question with three choices. When the participant selects a choice, she branches to the next level. The process continues until the participant achieves the goal or reaches a dead end.

Decision tree engine models are limited in that they cannot determine how events occur in relation to other events. For example, a decision made in one division of the company within a decision tree engine will have no bearing on the other divisions of the company (even though, in reality, different divisions affect one another all the time).

Because of this, these models are best suited for use with rule-based and goal-driven simulations, where there is a specific goal that must be reached. A simulation that teaches employees what happens in a stable, controlled environment when different chemicals are mixed together, for example, is a good use of a decision tree model. Not many outside factors would come into play as several chemicals are added together to produce one reaction.

Some extremely powerful simulations have been built using decision tree engines. Emergency room doctors and nurses use decision tree simulations to learn how to correctly diagnose medical conditions and take critical actions immediately after a patient arrives at the ER.

State Models are more complex than

simple decision engines. Instead of merely allowing employees to navigate from one pre-determined "path" to another, state models allow employees to jump from a decision point to entirely different outcomes (or states). Within a state model, every decision or movement, however minute, has the potential to influence the overall outcome of the simulation. State models offer a far more realistic experience than simple decision trees or spreadsheets, because they are not constrained to pre-determined paths. Instead, depending on the changes made in the current state (inputs an employee provides, external variables, and data generated by the model), the employee jumps to a different state (or level). This gives the simulation a more realistic feel, since the results of the same behaviors in real life can change from minute to minute.

Responsive Engines are the most powerful and best models of real-world behaviors. A responsive engine evaluates multiple decisions made by the participant and combines them with external conditions to produce both task and system feedback.

Task feedback relates to a decision or action that a participant or team performs on a specific task. *System feedback* provides insights to how the decisions and actions made at the task level impact the entire system.

These engines are best-suited for "real-world," complex situations that involve many factors and deal with randomness and uncertainty on a large scale.

When modeling the dynamics and causal connections of a business, a responsive engine is the best solution. The MBA simulation, presented as a case study throughout this book, was built on a responsive engine because of the need for an environment in which students could examine the impacts that their decisions had across all areas of a business and across various regions and product lines.

Common questions regarding models

Can a model be built to reflect our unique business?

Yes! This is the most common question that those considering simulations ask. The modeling process will work on any business of any size in any industry. Models have been built for projects as relatively simple as a Balanced Scorecard[21] and as complex as a multinational, multibillion-dollar corporation.

While it is possible to reflect any business, the success of any unique model largely depends on the abilities and choices of the modelers. Simulation development is an art form that requires expertise in business disciplines (accounting, marketing, operations, finance, human resources, supply chains, etc.), information systems, systems thinking, mathematics, and technology.

Who in our company needs to be involved in building the model?

There are many ways to gain valuable insights into a business when constructing a simulation model. Often, the training department staff members serve as subject matter experts working directly with an external simulation modeler. Managers and/or executives are also often asked to provide strategic visions for the company and validation of the final product.

Before the modeling process begins, the business modeler should ask a series of questions to understand what is important for employees to learn, what important information currently is available to employees, and which aspects of the business the employees can control. His or her goal is to determine how the business works and how different controls affect the business metrics across areas. Any unique aspects of the business must be included in addition to the standard parts. For example, in many businesses a layoff or reduction in staffing will slow production as remaining employees take on more responsibilities and worry about job security. The scope and relevance of this scenario for the specific business must be captured by the business modeler in order to produce a realistic simulation model.

After the initial round of discussions, the modeler and in-house modeling team create a working prototype for review by the content experts in different areas of the company.

As an added benefit, business staff members involved in the modeling process often gain a deeper understanding of the relationships between functional areas and how their business operates at every level. The business modeling process is one of the most rewarding parts of creating or validating the worth of a simulation.

What questions need to be answered in order to create a model?

First, what key aspects of the business do the employees need to understand? Consider the successful and/or competent employees in the areas that will participate in the training. What do they know that makes them valuable? What are the most common mistakes that the future participants are currently making? The model should demonstrate as many of these elements as possible—the right behaviors as well as the mistakes.

Second, what are important measurements for the relevant business parts? For example, if your business' goal is to improve inventory management, what information is available to help employees track and better manage inventory? How do you measure whether a manager is doing a good job? What financial or sales metrics attract your executives' focus? The measurements that matter to your everyday business should be included in the model.

Third, what essential aspects of your business can employees control? For example, can they change inventory levels, and is that important to the goals of the proposed training? Can they directly impact the cost of goods sold (or services sold)? Can they add or remove staff, and is that important? Can they change commission levels for salespeople, and is that important? Any elements that are essential to modeling the business as a systemic whole should be included the model.

Do models replicate the real world?

After examining simulations that *too* closely model the real world and simulations that model very little, our advice is to seek an optimal balance. Simulations that too closely model the real world are not only costly, but they are difficult to test and maintain and can impede a participant's learning by creating excessive complexity. A simulation that does not resemble the business closely enough makes it difficult to transfer learned skills to the workplace and fails to engage the learners.

Questions to help select the right model

These questions may seem simple, but if you really consider and apply the answers when you select a simulation model, you'll be more certain to make the right decision.

- Does the simulation feel and look like reality?
- Does it do what it is supposed to in terms of representing the workplace environments of the learners?
- Does the simulation respond in the way the real world would respond to employees' inputs?
- Does the technology or tool provide your business with the most cost-effective reach while achieving the appropriate level of richness?
- Does the simulation feature easy-to-use tools or computer engines to evaluate employees' responses?
- Does the model allow the learners to focus on their training goals rather than expending time and effort in the logistics of the simulation?

Interfaces

There are many approaches to building input interfaces. The goal for those who are interested in developing business simulations is to find one that will create the right environment for learning.

Some simulation interfaces attempt to mirror the real-world organization's information system, like an instrument panel or dashboard. Inputs, charts, or dials look like those used in the actual business environment. By contrast, some abstract interfaces look nothing like the real world. Simulation participants may input financial decisions into a web-based form that does not at all look like the actual line items and formatting of their real financial statements.

Which is better? It's best to do both.

Be as realistic as possible when you know that the interface can be cost-effectively created. For example, include exact replicas of your company's financial statements and management reports. However, when teaching a process or complex skill, don't attempt full realism. First, it costs too much, and second, the learner spends too much time trying to literally relate the simulation to the real environment and is more likely to lose interest.

Define the Simulation Time Frames

Wouldn't it be great if you could fast-forward a few months or years and evaluate the impact your decisions will have on your business? That is exactly what an engine-based simulation does, accelerating time in such a way that employees gain valuable and almost-immediate insights into the effects of their decisions. The simulation can make vast calculations, crunching reams of data so quickly that participants don't have to wait months or years to see the results of their decisions.

How does it work? For simplicity's sake, we will refer to one decision-making period within a simulation and the "jump forward" in time associated with it as a *round*.

A typical simulation process goes something like this:

In the first round, the learner completes all of the tasks assigned to him and submits his decisions. Instantly (or almost instantly, depending on the training schedule), the simulation advances to the next round, and the learner sees the impact of the decisions he made.

If the learner made good decisions, the company will be better off at the beginning of Round Two than it was at the beginning of Round One. If not, the employee will have re-evaluate the numbers, charts, and other performance feedback from the simulation in order to discover which decisions didn't pan out as he had hoped.

If the employee discovers in Round Two what her mistakes were, she can make several choices geared toward correcting the problems. Once Round Two is complete and the third round begins, the employee will receive more automated feedback regarding her new decisions. If her decisions during Round Two turned out well, she will continue trying to make good decisions as the simulation progresses into subsequent rounds.

Any executive knows that the only thing worse than making a costly mistake or bad decision is failing to learn from it. Many real-world employees, however, don't see the effects of their decisions on their businesses for weeks, months, or years–if at all. As a result, when reflecting on why they made a particular decision, employees often can't remember the circumstances or what motivated them to make a choice. Simulations eliminate this problem by condensing extended time periods into a matter of hours or days.

Simulations come with various time options. A simulation *time limit* refers to how many rounds a simulation goes through before it ends, and how much real-world time each round represents. A simulation might run for the equivalent of two years, or five, or even twenty.

A round may encompass a month, a year, or five years. However long you decide to make the simulation, when it's over, it's over. When a simulation's time limit ends, the participant receives her final numbers, which depict how her company did. She can make no further decisions without restarting the simulation.

An imposed time limit prevents simulated companies from becoming so powerful they stop being reflective of the real world. For example, if a participant works for a mid-sized company but grows his simulated business into a multinational colossus, the lessons cease to reflect the typical growth of a company.

The round limit appropriate for your business' learning needs will depend on a variety of factors. If you want your simulation to be as realistic as possible, consider how long participants stay in the positions for which they currently are training. Does it typically take two or three years before a worker is promoted? Or, is the worker in a career position that could last until retirement?

Some simulations run without time limits. In these cases, participants can choose to progress as far into the future as they wish and face more challenges. Simulations can be configured so that events—such as the opening of a new market or advances in technology—will occur at random times. The longer one plays the simulation, the more events he may experience. This option, of course, usually works best in more responsive simulations where the challenges and changes aren't scripted.

The "re-do" options

Engine-based simulations also often come with the option to "re-do" previous rounds or decisions. Using this capability, a learner can make a horrible mistake, see the outcome, and then go back and try another way. Unlike the real world, where once a decision is implemented there is no undoing it, simulations enable employees to correct mistakes. This way, participants see and begin to understand the complexity of a single decision on a variety of business processes, while also learning how to avoid making more mistakes in the future. The chance to re-do decisions becomes vital when an employee makes a company-destroying decision. When this occurs, the rest of the simulation experience can be negatively impacted because instead of learning, the participant spends much of her time trying to fix an unfixable situation.

For example, early in a simulation, an employee chooses to expand his business into Asia. However, he fails to realize that his organization has neither the financing nor the necessary resources to do so. In the next round, the learner's company has very little money—so little, in fact, that he can't afford to buy the materials required to make products. Even if the employee were subsequently to withdraw from Asia, the capital is already lost and the company is effectively bankrupt. As there is no "game over" in a simulation, the employee would have to proceed with a dysfunctional company. He would no longer be able to hire more workers, build new products, or even manufacture the company's existing lines. How will this help the participant learn anything during the rest of the simulation?

This simulation option obviously has drawbacks, as well. The ability to undo and re-do decisions can lead to an "addiction" to making the right choices. If a choice doesn't pan out as planned, for instance, the learner can re-do it over and over again until she achieves the perfect outcome. Within the simulation, this sometimes leads to building businesses with no average or wrong choices. This hinders the learning process because users neither learn how to deal with negative situations nor to "climb out of a hole" that they have created—two essential skills in business.

After all, there is no "re-do" button in real life.

International Electronics Company
TECHNOLOGY and TOOLS

Because IEC's training simulation was classroom-based, the designers created tools that tracked individual performance and supported the delivery of content.

For this training program, specific tools included:

Competency checklists–Forms were provided to each individual at the beginning of every round. Employees used them to evaluate their own competencies, as well as those of their teammates.

Customer evaluation forms–Each team would receive cumulative feedback at the conclusion of the simulation, based on the same competencies.

Group debriefing checklists–Customers provided teams with feedback on what they liked and disliked about the sales process after each client interview.

Team debriefing checklists–Each day, teams recapped and summarized what worked and what didn't, and then determined what they would do differently next time.

Action plans–Individuals immersed in the simulation would create personal action plans to help them remedy skill gaps discovered during the competency checklist process.

Regis University
MOTIVATORS

Motivating MBA students to participate in their simulation was a challenge for the University staff.

Initially, Regis' MBA faculty believed that students would be excited to change the pace of the program and compete in an on-line simulation. For the most part, they found the opposite to be true. Students worried that the simulation would identify their weaknesses or destroy their perfect grade-point averages, worried they would not be able to figure out how to run the multi-billion dollar business, and the list went on.

The failure of the initial round of the university capstone course was a perfect example of what can happen when decision-makers overlook critical steps of the SIMTEC model. In this case, Regis made incorrect assumptions about students' initial motivations, underestimated the impact of their negative emotions and fears, and didn't adequately motivate the students before the simulation began.

To improve the simulation, RLS went back to the model and reviewed all the top design elements: Pre-Simulation Objectives, Setting Goals, Working in Teams, and Managing the Emotional Throttle.

PRE-SIMULATION OBJECTIVES

The first few groups of students went into the simulation without information about the experience, the objectives of the simulation, or what would be expected of them. On top of that, they were not sure how their performance would be evaluated and how it would affect their grades. For the typically results-driven, highly competitive MBA student, earning an A was paramount.

To address this issue, RLS created a simulation Welcome Package. It contained a Mercury Shoes commercial, testimonials and helpful hints from students and professors, a Mercury shoes annual report, market analysis report, product and service descriptions, and three years of historical financial data for the fictional company. Regis University's dean provided incoming students with clear objectives and expectations.

These proactive steps seemed to lessen Regis students' fears to essential nervousness.

SETTING GOALS

As the simulation rounds progressed, students' motivational levels deteriorated. The simulation lacked clearly defined goals and milestones. As a result, students were frustrated because they did not know if they were succeeding. To address this issue, the following goals and milestones where created:

Performance Indexes–a series of key indicators were generated and presented each round. These indexes provided students a single-number overall evaluation of how they and their teammates performed.

Trends Reports–various reports compared actual results and forecasted results to help students think through setting future-oriented targets.

Management Reports–various management reports from each business unit provided students with a snapshot and historical information of the impact their decisions were having in individual areas.

Faculty Evaluations–faculty members established deadlines, to the day and hour, for teams to complete tasks for each round. When students "closed the books" and submitted their final decisions for a particular round, faculty reviewed the team's inputs and offered Socratic–style questions and ideas using an on-line bulletin board.

Team Debriefs–debriefs mostly helped to unify the teams. The objective was to get teams to discuss openly their successes and missteps, and to evaluate their companies' performances. In doing so, they would discover their dependencies and serve as coaches to each other. The result was a more confident team.

CREATING TEAMWORK AND TEAMBUILDING OPPORTUNITIES

Teamwork was not a problem in the simulation. In order for the students to accomplish all the tasks provided, they had to work in teams.

Teambuilding, however, proved to be a serious issue for some teams. Since students were located all over the country and could not meet in person, it required creativity to get them to work together.

A few times, students requested to "fire" other members of their teams. One enlightening instance occurred when a single individual asked for permission to fire his *entire* team. The faculty member wisely counseled him to try to work with the others to resolve issues and problems. At the end of the week, when the team completed their tasks and "closed the books," a turn of events occurred. The individual who wanted to fire the rest of the team had made seriously bad decisions—mainly because he elected not to work with the others on his team. As a result, the team asked for permission to fire the individual. Now that's humbling!

The simulation modeled the real world so well that faculty reported being able to identify which teams would fail and which would succeed by watching how well they worked together as a team.

Regis University developed a variety of solutions to address the teamwork and teambuilding elements. They established conference calls, on-line discussion groups, and general guidelines. However, the best solution came in the reminders from faculty that "In the real world you do not always get a chance to select your team or switch members when you feel like it, so figure it out."

EMOTIONAL THROTTLE

Just like in the real world, many factors contribute to making a simulation stressful. Some stressors were intentionally designed into the simulation, and others evolved as students ran their business. The Regis University team took about six months of constant adjusting to find the right balance.

The first emotional issue related to the Pre-Simulation objectives. The students wanted everything clearly laid out. What is the goal? How much money should we make in this division? What is the right amount of inventory to carry? What percentage of market share should we shoot for in Europe? How much money should we spend in marketing? Exactly what do you want my role to be and how should I do it?

To create a manageable environment as close as possible to the real world, the Regis faculty and RLS staff settled on the following:

1) Faculty assigned teams to create a mix of skill areas, but it was up to team members to further identify strengths and weaknesses.

2) Teams needed to organize themselves into the structure they thought would best serve the business (i.e. hierarchy by function, managers of product lines, managers of regions).

3) Typical information that would be available in any company would be given to the students (company overview and history, financial and management reports, product and service descriptions, and various market and industry analysis). Additionally, various hints and instructions were added to the many tasks that students needed to complete each week. However, over time clues were reduced or removed, because the students were given too much data and were no longer challenged to think.

2.5 ENVIRONMENT

Halo II, a multiplayer video game by Microsoft, grossed $125 million the first day it was released. The sixth Harry Potter book sold 8.9 million copies in twenty-four hours. The movie *Spider Man* grossed $114 million on its opening weekend. What do these three things have in common? They all have a strong environment, including a powerful storyline and a well-designed flow that make people want to experience more to find out what will happen next.

Just like a book or a movie, a business simulation's *storyline* establishes the plot and engages audience interest. The storyline helps participants identify with the characters and the situations. They become emotionally engaged in decisions and examine their actions and alternative responses. In short, a great storyline pulls observers in and makes the situation feel real.

Flow is a word simulation creators use to define a successful environment. The flow defines how employees will interact and be guided through rounds and tasks. It sets the pace, allowing participants to stop, re-group, evaluate, and start again in the right places.

A business simulation's environment defines how participants will progress through a simulation and what will happen at each stage. The questions and ideas presented here will help you mold the requirements of how the simulation will look and feel—whether you're designing a facilitator-led, on-line simulation or a computer-based simulation.

As we saw in the last section, most simulations have multiple rounds or stages that employees must go through. The decisions or actions made by employees in a particular round will have some type of consequence in the following levels. These two requirements define flow, navigation, and feedback points.

Here is a list of questions to consider when selecting or building the simulation environment:

- Is the simulation guided or exploratory?
- Is there a primary objective and/or milestones?
- How and when is feedback provided?
- How and when is debriefing provided?
- Will self-evaluations and group evaluations be integrated?
- Will competencies be integrated?
- Are there winners and losers?
- At what level should the emotional throttle be set?
- Will participants go through the simulation in teams or as individuals?

Develop a Simple and Realistic Storyline

In order for the simulation to be meaningful, the storyline needs to be realistically tied to the business. It should provide motivation for active learning and reflection by encompassing engaging situations that the participant must address. It also needs to be simple and easy to follow.

Why is a storyline important?

A storyline is important because it serves as a framework for developing content and technology. The storyline defines the structure and flow of the simulation, as well as the content that will engage participants. A well-defined storyline will let trainers know in advance what supporting materials they should provide before, during, and after the simulation, and how and when feedback and debriefing sessions will best fit into the schedule.

What does a storyline include?

A complete storyline should:

- Define the scope of the industry
- Include market size and conditions
- Describe the potential for growth, expected milestones and any exogenous effects the economy may have on the industry, market, and/or company
- Depict the history and current (initial) state of the company

What else should be considered?

- Before beginning the simulation, do participants understand the goal and their role in achieving the goal?
- Do participants understand the context of their situation— how the company got to where it is and its current condition?
- Does the storyline gradually build from round to round?
- Does the storyline include characters or have roles with whom the participants can identify?
- Is the storyline realistic?
- Does the storyline provide opportunities for exploration and debriefing?
- At the end of the simulation, will the participants view the simulation as relevant to their job and goals?
- Does the storyline focus on your business strategy?

Define the Flow

Video games, books, and movies all have a flow. They usually start simply, establishing the characters and the storyline. Various twists and turns emerge gradually as the story progresses. The story draws participants in deeper, increasing their distraction and emotional engagement. Only when the audience is fully engaged do the connections and big-picture revelations start to make sense.

Let's explore a few questions that you should consider when reviewing or building the flow for a simulation. Keep your storyline in mind when reviewing these questions.

Are there multiple rounds? If so, how many activities are there and how long does it take (on average) to complete an activity? This will help you determine how much time an individual will need to successfully go through the simulation.

Do the rounds build on each other? Participants with little foundational knowledge will have a difficult time with a simulation that starts at a level beyond their abilities. Be sure to know your participants' knowledge and skill levels, then design the simulation progression accordingly.

How much clock time will participants have from beginning to end of a round? Participants need the sense that they have a fair chance to consume the data and other information the simulation provides, consider it, and then apply it to the tasks they have been assigned. Too much to do in too little time will evoke negative emotions–fear, anger, cynicism–and damage the simulation's impact.

Allow for times of reflection

A good simulation will have a lot going on within it, just like the real world that the simulation is modeling. Participants immersed in a high-impact simulation should be forced to contend with an array of various inputs, distractions, and feedback at the same time.

Given the rapid pace of such simulations, participants often need time between rounds to take a breath, reflect on what happened during the previous round, and prepare a strategy for the next phase.

There are two effective techniques for providing this time. The first is to feature debriefing sessions at the conclusion of each round. Alternately, many simulation providers have found it beneficial to have participants write a memo explaining their decisions and results in the last round and of the simulation thus far, and an outline of their objectives for the remainder of the simulation.

Keep it relevant

To keep participants interested and engaged, your simulation must be relevant to their jobs. As you think about the flow of your business simulation, consider implementing a few of these techniques:

- **Have participants complete an expectations questionnaire** before they start the simulation. An expectations questionnaire is a powerful tool to ensure that the participants clearly define what they hope to get out of the simulation. The questionnaire usually contains about 10-20 open- and close-ended questions. Often, the objectives of the simulation are re-stated on the questionnaire so participants can reference them as they answer the questions.

- **Use a competency matrix.** Competency profiles are becoming popular in many organizations because they provide a common language to define requirements in order to assess individuals. A competency defines the knowledge, skill, or attitude that is needed to effectively perform an on-the-job activity. A competency matrix is a self-assessment tool (paper-based or electronic) that lists the competencies taught by the simulation. Prior to beginning the simulation, participants indicate how well they know or can perform a specific competency (e.g. awareness, literacy, fluency, mastery). After each round or major milestone in the simulation, the participant once again indicates his knowledge or expertise. Thus, as the participant goes through the simulation he is continually reminded of what it takes to perform a specific job.

- **Use integrated assessments.** Threading assessments throughout the simulation keeps the simulation relevant. A well-written pre-assessment serves as a performance benchmark, a reminder of the simulation's objectives, and hopefully as a motivator to keep the participant's interest through the simulation. After each round, a knowledge check assessment reinforces the relevancy of the simulation and is an excellent source for the simulation facilitator to review and give feedback. If possible, the final assessment should be a 360-degree assessment in which teammates, observers, facilitators or others can provide feedback to the participant.

Allow Opportunities to Explore

Exploration within a simulation allows employees to see the effects of various actions as they relate to their business. This has advantages over experimentation in the real world, because in a simulation, the effects of each choice are transparent. In addition, because a simulated company exists only in a virtual environment, employees can make riskier choices without real-world consequences.

In reality, an employee's decision may not directly have a negative impact on his own job, but a worker in another department may deal with the ramifications of that decision for weeks. In a simulation, by contrast, the employee can see and feel responsible for everything that goes on interdepartmentally, allowing him to see and analyze the effects of his actions. This type of simulated environment is *systemic* in nature.

In relation to simulations, systemic environments are those in which employees are immersed in a setting that constantly changes, with non-linear consequences for decisions made during the learning process. While linear environments, like decision tree models, involve simple chains of cause and effect, in a systemic environment multiple factors are taken into account based on each decision an employee makes.

Obviously, the real world is a systemic environment that is neither simple nor predictable. Unforeseeable outside events affect the system every day. Every action and decision has both intended and unintended consequences.

That said, it is important to note that although uncontrollable forces may shape the outcomes of our choices within systemic environments, a well-educated and informed choice will afford a better chance of succeeding than one based purely on guesswork.

If a manager must cut payroll by twenty percent and chooses to lay off ten people, the intended consequence is that payroll decreases to an acceptable level. However, an unintended consequence of this action is that morale drops so low that ten more people leave. Suddenly, there is a deficit in productivity, goals are not reached, and the remaining employees are being pushed so hard that their morale drops even further.

Exploration

Business leaders stay awake at night, thinking about the fact that people throughout their organizations are making seemingly small business decisions every day that will have far-reaching consequences. The workers who make these decisions, on the other hand, may never see or know how they impacted the overall well-being of the organization.

Systemic simulations help close this gap; by participating, employees experience a bird's eye view of the intended and unintended consequences of each action.

An experienced manager may anticipate that morale will drop as a result of the firings. Foreseeing this potential problem, she could adjust her decision and only let five people go. Although she has only reduced payroll by ten percent, low morale quickly prompts five additional people to quit their jobs, bringing payroll down again to the desired twenty percent cut.

How would an experienced manager know to do this? How would she know to expect several resignations after the firings? Perhaps because she has faced the same situation before and learned from her mistakes. Or maybe she gained this experience and insight through a workplace simulation.

Just as a master archer becomes accomplished only after years of practice and exploration–learning over time how to predict how far the wind will blow an arrow off course and how to adjust aim to compensate for such a variable–an employee who is given the opportunity to try, make mistakes, and try again until she experiences some degree of success can learn to foresee potential problems related to her decisions and adjust those decisions accordingly.

Simulations also allow employees to immediately put into practice the lessons learned during the simulation. Participants can use skills from one round during subsequent rounds. Each time they go through a simulation round, ideas and knowledge are imbedded deeper within their minds, so that when the unexpected does occur in real life, simulation graduates are better prepared for it.

A pilot in training, for example, does not quit after one crash landing in a flight simulator. Instead, he learns from the experience and uses that knowledge during his next landing attempt. The same can be said for business employees. Running a simulated business into the ground simply provides some valuable experiences and lessons to incorporate the next time.

Integrating an exploration element into a class-based simulation

Often, classroom simulations integrate exploration through group debriefing sessions or through a Socratic discussion between participants and the facilitator. During a debriefing session, participants talk about the decisions they made during the simulation and the corresponding outcomes. In doing so, participants begin to explore new ideas and approaches that they may not have considered previously–or that they didn't try during the actual round.

Integrating an exploration element into a technology-based simulation

This requires either a responsive modeling engine or an engine based on AI (artificial intelligence). These engines are designed to evaluate and provide feedback for the quality of thinking across many integrated decisions.

Engines vary in terms of types and the detail of the feedback each type provides, but in general, most provide at least simple cause and effect of insights based on participant decisions. As you can imagine, an evaluation engine combined with debriefing can create a very powerful environment for exploration.

International Electronics Company
ENVIRONMENT

Because their goal was to replicate the real-life sales environment, IEC's training team decided to use a classroom environment for their simulation. The classroom allowed team members to interact directly with each other and with their "customers." Since personal interaction is such a crucial part of the sales process, the simulation needed to provide as much face-to-face communication as possible.

Combining the simulation with a classroom environment provided real-world, emotionally-charged learning. To encourage realistic interaction, multiple break-out rooms were arranged for customers and sales teams to meet privately when needed. There were also telephones, internet connections, and board-room style areas for meetings.

STORYLINE

In a simulation, the story shouldn't be so complicated that it distracts teams from their purpose, but it needs to be complex enough to allow different teams to approach the issue in

---

different ways. IEC's storyline was designed to be simple, but realistic.

During their simulation, teams called on a customer who needed an order filled. If they engaged the customer in conversation, the sales team would discover other sales opportunities within the customer's organization. During the simulation, teams could continue to inquire about the customer's needs, earning introductions to several senior employees. The customer's decision-making committee was in the process of selecting a vendor to service a large business expansion opportunity. Only one team would be awarded that business.

DESIGN DECISIONS

In addition to making decisions about the environment and the storyline, IEC made the following design decisions:

Build multiple simulation rounds that gradually introduce and build upon previously mastered selling skills.

Create a "boot camp" atmosphere that is mentally intense but that balances competition and teamwork.

Provide clear communication for managers throughout the company about the process and the outcomes of new-hire sales training before, during, and after the training program.

Indoctrinate new-hire sales people in the "company way," further reinforcing the vision and values.

Conclude the simulation so that one team wins the business and the rest lose.

Thread competencies throughout the simulation to help with self-evaluation.

Debrief after each round–including peer, group, and customer debriefs.

Incorporate "Golden Threads" throughout the simulation, turning key concepts into reoccurring themes. Golden Threads for IEC's program included:

- Teach unique sales process
- Focus on company-specific services
- Impart operating knowledge of internal resources

- Focus on a consultative approach to selling
- Migrate inside sales toward outside sales (teamwork)
- See red flags as opportunities
- Create leverage and differentiation in the sale
- Learn realistic self-evaluation
- Excite participants about working at IEC

These storyline and design decisions served as the framework for identifying and developing content. In addition, they helped IEC determine the optimal technology solution.

Regis University
ENVIRONMENT

To create the environment, Regis University decided to make their simulation look and feel like a real company portal. Industry news, market data, and stock quotes all added to the realism of the site.

To ensure teams were able to learn from their experiences and demonstrate change, the training team created a series of rounds with debriefing points. Each round featured a unique web homepage which was activated on the appropriate week. The new webpage appeared on a team's simulation portal with all the data–including the team's financial, production, and sales data–generated from the results of the model following the previous round. Faculty feedback provided additional qualitative guidance regarding how to move forward.

Model designers developed the following list of design ideas to create the storyline, determine the flow, and create an environment that modeled the real world. Ultimately, each these design ideas drove the decisions made for building the Technology and Tools and authoring the Content.

DESIGN DECISIONS

Incorporate a simulation component that would give students practical business experience by allowing them to assume the role of a senior executive. Allow students to serve in senior-level roles within the hypothetical company featured in the simulation.

Allow for both synchronous and asynchronous communication among students and between faculty and students.

Include teamwork opportunities that model a real-life senior management team in a real-life business environment, and provide team members with an array of opportunities to make decisions about strategic issues.

Provide faculty with both qualitative and quantitative data on student performance, participation, and collaboration within teams. As teams prepare annual or quarterly budgets, for example, or make marketing and hiring decisions, faculty members need to receive updated reports on the progress.

Minimize assumptions about students' pre-requisite knowledge, yet include simulation content in their major business disciplines: sales, marketing, finance, operations, and human resources.

Integrate the impact of government policy and economics.

Require decisions about human resources to support business strategy.

Incorporate ongoing decisions about operations, finance, marketing, and law and ethics.

Provide feedback to students within a simulated, systemic framework, about the intended and unintended implications and consequences of their strategic decisions and actions.

Simulate a business that includes both a service component and some form of supply-chain and manufacturing component, as well as an international market reach into at least three continents.

Allow faculty to conduct an assessment of each section's MBA course background and business experiences in order to tailor the content of the pre-simulation portion of the course to students' needs.

Plan for ongoing updates and maintenance of course content, as well as changes to the hypothetical business that students will run while immersed in the simulation.

2.6 CONTENT

As we discussed in the last section, the environment defines how participants experience a simulation. Content, on the other hand, defines what they do during the simulation.

The environment defines the storyline, the flow (rounds), and the opportunities to explore alternatives. The content dimension focuses on what needs to be created for the storyline, what tasks and supporting materials need to be created for the flow, and what content needs to be provided to encourage employees to explore.

Think of the environment as the outside of a house, whether it is a ranch, a bungalow, a Victorian, or a farmhouse. The frame defines the structure, the style, and the form. The content is like the furniture and the decorations inside. Ideally, they should relate to the structure–functional modern furniture in a bungalow or Louis XIV antiques in a Victorian mansion. The content makes the house interesting and comfortable; it defines the spaces and gives the rooms a purpose. The content and the environment of a simulation are different components, but in the most successful cases they are designed and work together.

There are numerous content design elements that need to be understood in order to determine whether your simulation:

- Provides the right amount of supporting materials
- Provides sufficient feedback, coaching, and debriefing
- Allows for exploration and problem solving
- Integrates an appropriate amount of gaming components
- Contains a reference library to accommodate both novice and expert participants

Content, framework, and technology all interrelate. As you make decisions about your simulation content, they will have a direct impact on both framework and technology. Therefore, it is important for you to think about all three as a system and, as a system, how they meet the participants' needs and address the business strategy.

There are several key questions to consider when thinking about the content dimension:

- **Purpose**–Does the content and design support the learning objectives? That is, after the participants go through the simulation, will they feel like the experience was relevant to their job?

- **Richness**–Does the simulation design support the desired performance level? Are you shooting for the mastery level, or will fluency do? (You don't need to over-engineer the simulation to help participants achieve a mastery level if fluency will be enough to achieve the business strategy.)

- **Feedback**–The most powerful and important simulation content decision you will make concerns the type, frequency, and amount of feedback participants will get. Too much feedback becomes unintelligible noise; too little feedback leaves participants floundering. Do the simulation, facilitators, and coaches provide meaningful and timely feedback?

- **Supporting Materials**–Does the simulation offer enough background information to guide the participants appropriately? Consider what supporting materials participants will need before, during, and after the simulation. Supporting materials are essential to ensuring that participants feel confident before starting the simulation and that they don't get frustrated during it.

Define the Purpose: Facts vs. Skills

There are two primary content types: fact-based content and skill-based content.

Awareness and literacy-level performance is best achieved through *fact-based content*. Why? Because fact-based content is linear in nature (books, lectures, assembly instructions for your new barbecue grill, etc.) and often is used to guide an employee step-by-step through the learning process. Fact-based content has a pre-determined path.

Skill-based content, by contrast, is best suited for helping employees achieve higher levels of performance, such as mastery or anticipatory. Skill-based content has no pre-determined path and is adaptive in nature. Such content allows people to take various facts and knowledge learned through fact-based content and pull them together to develop, try, and master new skills.

One difference between the performance outcomes of fact- and skill-based content can best be expressed by comparing book- and lecture-based learning with simulation-based learning.

Think back to your high-school and college years. Remember those late-night cram sessions, when you spent hours memorizing information in order to recall it during the next morning's test? Once the test was completed, you probably never had to think about those facts again. You used your short-term memory to load the data, but there was no incentive for your brain to retain information once the test is over.

By contrast, when going through a simulation, knowledge and skills are used over and over in various ways until they are learned well past the short-term memory. A person within a simulation can't simply memorize a few facts until the test is completed, because there is no test.

Fact- and Skill-based Learning

John wants to start his own business, so he reads a self-help book on the subject. He opens a shop, but quickly discovers that running a business is more complicated than the book indicated. Thanks to his readings, John has sufficient knowledge to perform certain simple tasks, but he doesn't posses the necessary skills required to do the more complicated things he needs to do in order for the business to succeed.

Why? John learned about running a business by reading a book, which is a form of fact-based learning. More often than not, it is difficult for people to take knowledge learned through fact-based learning and transfer that knowledge to perform actual complex tasks without first being immersed in an environment in which they can practice those skills.

Of course, it would have been preferable (and more effective) if John had read the self-help book first and then worked for someone's small business for a few months before starting his own. John would have had an opportunity to practice all of the skills he would eventually need to apply within his own business while under the tutelage of an experienced shop owner who could correct any mistakes John made and help fill in any knowledge gaps that John had.

In order to transform knowledge (knowing how to do something) to complex skills (actually being able to physically perform a complex task), one must *practice*! While this is obvious with some physical activities, like swinging a golf club or driving a standard transmission, more complex emotional and mental skills present a less obvious but more difficult challenge.

This common-sense application is evident in at least one profession; most restaurateurs learn their chosen business by working in a restaurant before they open their own. Such a scenario demonstrates a form of skill-based learning within an environment that is constantly changing and that requires the actual application of knowledge and the transfer of knowledge to skills.

Ensure Richness and Reach

Content drives the richness of a simulation. There is a process to learning, with fact-based learning serving as the base upon which skill-based learning is built.

Skill-based learning is best used in business simulations where employees already have the building blocks acquired through linear learning. If a participant does not possess fact-based knowledge, he is likely to stumble through a simulation without ever fully understanding why or how he is performing certain tasks.

In other words, a simulation allows you to use and hone skills, but there must be a basis upon which to build. If you went through a simulation on keeping tax records without knowing the basics of taxes, then you wouldn't know which numbers to put where. You would not able to fully understand the results of your work, because you would have no context in which to place them. While you certainly would learn from the simulation, it would be more efficient to learn this foundational knowledge though linear learning first and engage in a simulation later.

Develop Reflective Feedback

One of the most important components of a simulation is feedback. Feedback can make your simulation work or cause it to be ineffective. The right feedback from the right sources at critical moments is essential.

Without feedback, employees might go through an entire simulation without ever stopping to think, "Why am I trying to solve this problem in this particular way?" or, "Are there better ways to handle this situation?"

Feedback not only helps employees understand the importance of their actions and guides them through the process of dealing with and solving problems, it also provides positive reinforcement for their victories and constructive feedback for their failures. It is crucial to the learning process because it reinforces newly acquired knowledge and forces employees to analyze their own actions and decisions. Through such analyses, lessons learned within a simulation are engrained in learners' minds to a far greater extent than they would be if they were simply read in a book.

In a simulation, there are two primary ways to supply feedback to trainees. The first is through a human facilitator or coach. The second is via technology. Both require a simulation framework to trigger when and what kind of feedback to provide. The design of these feedback methods and their timing is very critical to the success of the simulation. (Refer to the section on Design to learn more about feedback design considerations.)

If your simulation provides feedback through the human facilitator, consider that this is just one of the many hats the coach must wear. She is a guide who helps the employees comprehend the basic rules of the simulation so that they will spend their time learning the business lessons that the simulation intends to teach, rather than spending time trying to figure out the rules, format, and protocol of the simulation.

The Role of the "Coach"

A good coach doesn't just tell you what to do; he helps you discover success on your own. Socrates would have been a great simulation coach, with his artful method of asking questions. He found that the way we ask and perceive questions profoundly influences how the mind processes and searches for answers. The purest form of the teaching method that bears his name uses questioning techniques exclusively to guide the learner through the process. Learners acquire not only knowledge and skills, but the ability to think through problems and situations.

The role of a simulation coach is to get employees to question their ideas, their choices, and their results. Although there are some great self-guided simulations available, a business simulation should provide opportunities for a coach or facilitator to ask Socratic questions.

Simulation coaches are instrumental in gauging and controlling the "emotional throttle" of a class. If the simulation becomes too intense and learning is impeded because people are angry, the facilitator needs to step in and lend some assistance. While a certain amount of frustration on learners' parts is healthy and even desirable, tension that continues at an unhealthy level class after class should lead the facilitator to take action and make adjustments.

The facilitator must also act as a tour guide of the simulation by focusing learners' attention on specific aspects of the simulation. His role is to offer helpful hints and advice when participants get stuck, ensuring that everything runs smoothly and employees are free to explore and learn during their time within the simulation rather than worrying about unnecessary details.

A facilitator shouldn't give participants answers every time they get stuck. Instead, the facilitator should make employees question their own actions, reflect on what they have been doing, and urge them see the situation from a different angle. In this way, employees can discover the answers to their own questions. In Part Three, we will examine best practices for selecting and preparing facilitators.

The research of Hattie and Jaeger shows that the most powerful single contributor to achievement is feedback. The more feedback an employee receives, the more she will achieve.[22]

Also keep in mind that diverse feedback more effectively reinforces key skills being learned within the simulation.

Create Supportive Materials

Supporting materials serve as the glue between a simulation's activities and its storyline. These materials help to get participants into the proper mindset to perform the various activities required throughout the simulation.

There are three categories used to organize the various types of supporting materials: direct content, indirect content, and distracters. All three types are important components of the content featured in a simulation.

Direct content provides specific information that participants need to accomplish the various tasks within a simulation. For example, direct content may include historical financial data, company overviews, or market and competition analyses.

Indirect content provides employees with information that potentially could influence or impact their decisions within the simulation. For example, Regis's simulation for an athletic shoe company might feature "news" that provides the participants with insight into the political, economic, and social conditions of the country where the products are manufactured. This information might be helpful if employees make a decision to expand their business in that country.

Distracters have two primary goals. First, they teach participants to filter information and identify what is pertinent and what is not. Second, they increase the amount of stress employees experience during the simulation by creating events that take attention away from current tasks, burying them for a time with excess information.

Direct Content

Direct content is provided to individuals or teams, depending on how the simulation is set up. Direct content might appear in the form of a virtual e-mail, memo, or report. Each employee on a team or specific sub-groups of the team may receive different direct-content messages including stock reports, productivity reports, sales reports, etc.

Keep in mind when designing a simulation that direct content should always be presented as information of value. The source should not be questionable; reports and numbers should come from within the company or a trusted reporting source. The employee should be able to act on direct content without questioning or needing to verify.

Ideally, direct content should be given to participants before the simulation begins, so that they have time to review it and acquire a general knowledge of where they stand. This will save time and improve the simulation's efficiency.

Direct content–such as updates on stock ratings or information on the competition–should continue to flow to the participants as the simulation progresses. This material does not need to be labeled as "direct content," because it will have a natural place in the simulation. (If it arrives as a memo from the research department or a report from the marketing department, the content will be believable and more likely to be read and used.)

The rules of the simulation are also direct content. Everyone must follow these rules to ensure that the simulation runs smoothly. There are few experiences more frustrating in a simulation than having things go wrong because a participant did not follow directions. Sadly, this will happen from time to time despite your training team and coach's best efforts to prevent it.

Indirect Content

Indirect content is generalized and not employee- or team-specific. Indirect content includes information to which everyone participating in the simulation has access.

Whereas direct content contains facts produced by the simulation through the initial content design or after analysis of learners' choices, indirect content contains information about things that could possibly help or may waste valuable company time and resources.

Indirect content can take the form of a news story, an outside analysis of the market's future, or a report on stockholders' expectations. In terms of subject matter, indirect content might deal with a new company entering your area of the market, a natural disaster, a new product that the competition is releasing, political viewpoints in relation to your organization's products, or shortages in the raw materials needed to make your product.

Of course, some indirect content will have nothing to do with what employees are trying to achieve, and the design of the simulation may not take these events into account at all. For employees, the key to navigating successfully through a simulation is to accurately identify which information matters—and which does not.

Distracters

Every day of our lives, we are bombarded with information. Before we leave our houses in the morning, we might read the paper or watch the morning news. On the way to work, billboards and the radio fill our heads with more information. Once we get to work, there is daily mail to sort through, reports and memos to read, messages on our voice mail to listen to, meetings to attend, other employees to communicate with, and e-mail to review. In the midst of sorting information, we are constantly interrupted—by the telephone ringing while we race to finish a report or by a co-worker stopping by our office to chat about the latest company meeting.

In such a crowded environment, it is amazing that employees don't overload and quit functioning altogether. Yet somehow, most of us manage to filter through this bombardment and to perform productively in our work.

A complex simulation will include distracter messages to add to the richness and real-world nature of the participant's experience.

The difference between a distracter and relevant, key information may be a matter of perspective. Consider a news flash announcing the collapse of the U.S.S.R. A learner immersed in a simulation might receive a breaking-news headline that reads, "The U.S.S.R. is folding. Russia and several of its former members are expected to turn capitalistic." A short news story would follow.

Is this information relevant to the simulation and to what the participant is attempting to achieve? An employee with an eye for potential may see possibilities inherent to such a situation. In reality, the breakup of the U.S.S.R. fundamentally changed the landscape of the global business world. Suddenly there were new untapped markets. Research efforts began immediately, forming the basis for new marketing schemes. Budgets had to be revised to create the financial wherewithal for companies to expand past the Iron Curtain before the competition did so. There suddenly were nations of people without jobs; the labor pool was almost endless.

If this news flash went out to all employees immersed in a simulation, not everyone would act on the information. Some might not even notice the news flash in the cycle of news stories that popped up during the day. To further complicate matters, the information may have been hidden beneath other distracters.

In this way, distracters help simulations to more accurately reflect the real world.

Add Filters

A crucial skill for success in any business is the ability to filter information in a way that eliminates the noise and hones in on what's important. Thus, a simulation must possess the ability to develop learners' capacity to process and use information wisely by requiring them to filter a great deal of information in order to make their decisions. After all, that's the real world!

Meanwhile, workers also must filter interruptions continually in order to determine whether they are important or urgent and prioritize their work accordingly. A "to do" list is constantly shifting, for example, as new items are added, certain things become more important, and individual projects are finished. It is not unusual to have a number-one priority that has to be put off for several hours because of two or three smaller matters that jump up on the list and consume attention. This way, every worker spends much of the day jumping from task to task while re-prioritizing and filtering information and interruptions the entire time.

Interruptions

Interruptions are a regular part of the real world, and they're an integral part of a high-impact simulation, where participants encounter regular interruptions that distract them from the tasks at hand and force them to focus all of their attention on the pending emergency.

Simulations can incorporate the many real-world forms of interruptions, from urgent phone calls and e-mails to "drop ins" from a co-worker, to force employees to spread their focus among various tasks and to prioritize activities. A union strike, a factory fire, a war, a natural disaster, or a sudden dip in the stock market all are examples of such interruptions.

Simulations that incorporate interruptions are not only apt to more accurately reflect reality; they also help participants learn how to prioritize and multitask more efficiently.

Great business simulations reflect this reality. As a simulation participant works to create a budget report for her company, she might be alerted that there is a shortage of supplies to one of the company's branches that needs to be addressed immediately. After that, she might receive a news flash informing her that the Chinese government plans to open its borders to the product her company sells. Immediately, the employee begins typing a report detailing her ideas for entering this new market. After all of this, the employee finally returns to the task of working on the budgeting report—which now needs to be updated to reflect recent developments.

Although the presence of constant interruptions and new information within simulations won't teach employees how to work any faster in the real world, the feedback they receive and the results they experience *will* help them learn to work more efficiently by prioritizing tasks, while allowing enough flexibility to meet the demands of new, unanticipated needs.

The presence of constant interruptions and new information within simulations also helps trainees learn how to filter the important from the unimportant distracters. Some simulation events, for example, demand learners' immediate attention, just as they would in the real world. Others are distracters—and, as such, are irrelevant and can be safely ignored.

For simulation participants, the trick is to make a proper distinction between the two. How does an employee know, for example, which news stories to act on and which to ignore? How does he know how to make the distinction between irrelevant information and vital information that, if exploited properly, might lead to huge growth and profits for his company? He doesn't!

At first, this onslaught of information and interruptions may seem overwhelming to trainees, but as the simulation advances so will employees' capacities to filter out useless information and filter in what's important. How? If they choose to act on bad information, they will see the effects of their decision on the business in the next round of the simulation. As time passes and employees receive ongoing feedback on their progress, they will quickly learn how to discern important and unimportant information more efficiently and with greater precision.

Remember the emotional throttle? When considering interruptions, remember to strive to achieve a balance. Too much information and too many interruptions might overwhelm participants and lead to analysis-paralysis. Too little information or too few interruptions, by contrast, might de-motivate participants.

Gaming

It doesn't matter how old you are. From the time we are children to the time we become adults, we would rather be playing a game than sitting in a classroom. In simulations, gaming elements provide motivation, structure, defined goals, and a competitive environment for learning.

Despite the popularity of games, especially among the twenty-something set, there is some stigma attached to "learning games." Some more traditional learning advocates suggest that games aren't as effective at teaching knowledge and skills as are traditional classroom and book methods.

It's no wonder, then, that games are often misunderstood by businesspeople and that their benefits as learning tools are underappreciated.

However, simulations that include gaming elements such as scorekeeping, competition, and surprise variables (or distracters) can increase the entertainment value, effectiveness, and fun of the learning experience.

Furthermore, business simulations can include these gaming elements without losing the elements of effective teaching. In fact, a simulation's effectiveness as a learning tool often increases when gaming elements are incorporated, because participants get excited about what they are doing. And when they are "into" the simulation, they pay more attention, try harder, and are willing to put up with more frustration than they would be if they weren't fully engaged in the simulation experience.

Graphics and video games

In their infancy, simulations were somewhat mechanical in nature. They were meant to convey information by immersing the employee in an environment and featured only a bare minimum of graphics, exploration, and interactive design.

Over time, however, simulation designers discovered that if they incorporated elements of video games into their simulations, the business simulations tended to draw employees in more deeply, thus providing richer and more engaging learning experiences. Over time, this extra "eye candy" has become less of a perk and more of a necessity.

Research backs up this claim. Some industry experts believe high-quality graphics are essential, especially for young employees who have grown up playing video games.[23]

This makes sense. Better graphics help suspend disbelief. This means that employees are more likely to accept what is happening on the screen and treat it in a serious manner. There also is less of a chance that they will throw up their hands and say, "This doesn't reflect reality at all!" and walk off. Because simulations that incorporate elements of video games draw employees in more deeply, employees, in turn, are willing to deal with more frustration. This allows the simulation to push the employee harder to grasp new concepts and to acquire new knowledge.

Video

Content gaming elements also often involve video. Instead of dealing with computer-generated graphics, users immersed in these simulations interact with "real" people.

Despite being extremely engaging, the use of live actors portraying real people does have drawbacks. The cost to develop and maintain such a simulation typically is higher than other graphics options. In addition, actors can only be used for simple decision-tree simulations, because it would be impossible to script the infinite number of outcomes possible within AI-based simulations.

Having said that, video depictions of live actors can be particularly effective in simulations used within certain industries, such as law enforcement, medicine, and the military. Employees within these industries often deal with heightened situations in which a single decision can mean the difference between life and death. After all, would you want *your* future doctor training and learning his craft through the use of a pixilated cartoon?

Avatars are a video alternative to actors. Originating from the gaming and 3-D chat worlds, avatars are computer-based caricatures that can "interact" with participants. A commonly known (albeit annoying) avatar is the Microsoft Office Assistant "Clippy." More complex avatars based upon AI engines can be found in business simulations such as Virtual Leader from SimuLearn in Norwalk, CT. An AI-based avatar can respond to various participant responses.

International Electronics Company
CONTENT

During the initial design process, IEC realized that it already had solid content in the form of training presentations, e-learning, and other print resources that provided a good overview of the company's product and service offerings. Because the new sales hires still needed to know about these products and services, the team decided to leverage existing content and work it into the new program. A skill-based simulation would be used in conjunction with the existing legacy materials to relate the training back to the unique sales experience.

The original content provided the foundational information necessary to get participants to a literacy level of selling. The new skill-based content added a new layer of richness to the training. For example, a customer might provide a participant with specific information if he felt that the participant earned it during one of many meetings. If, however, the participant skipped the application of key skills, or did not appropriately apply a particular skill covered in separate knowledge-based training aspects, then information would be withheld—which could hurt a team's chance of later earning the business.

To further heighten participant tension, several distracters were provided that might take careless or less discerning participants down the wrong track. For example, throughout the simulation teams received e-mails from clients informing them about changes in the clients' situations or offering hints that the clients' needs are changing.

In addition, IEC set the scene for the simulation by providing participants with detailed background information. Before the simulation began, teams received information about their clients; this material was similar to what would be publicly available to any salesperson, including information on the size and financial health of the company, the basic business situation, and the background of the team's contact person.

The way that the content was presented to simulation participants was also carefully considered. The proper presentation can help enhance the realism of a simulation and engage participants from the beginning. In IEC's simulation, each participant received a binder with company and product information. They also received e-mails from their "clients" during the simulation. By incorporating information in different formats and from different sources, the designers were able to make the simulation feel more real.

Regis University
CONTENT

Because the Regis simulation was based on a new, totally fictional company, Regis needed to create a huge amount of content. The development team worked for months to create background information about the company, financial and management reports, analyst reports, a market analysis, and news articles about Mercury Shoes, the industry, and other events that might affect the students.

The content provided the foundation for the simulation by giving students the numbers and other financial data that they needed to make decisions, but it also gave the simulation texture and depth. Just like in the real world, news articles, radio reports, and other media offered valuable tidbits and distracting information. For example, early in the simulation students see a news story about the rising minimum wage in the Philippines and another about promising new technology that might allow

145

shoe companies to cheaply produce synthetic rubber. Based on these articles, and the rest of the content, students made decisions about how to run Mercury Shoes.

---

[13] Nosotro, Rit. *Bill Gates: Brought Simple Computing to the World.* 27 Oct. 2003 <http://www.hyperhistory.net/apwh/mast/ citation.htm>.

[14] Mager, R. F., and Peter Pipe. *Analyzing Performance Problems or "You Really Oughta Wanna."* Atlanta: Center for Effective Performance, 1997.

[15] Robinson, Dana Gaines, and James Robinson. *Performance Consulting: Moving Beyond Training.* San Francisco: Berrett-Koehler Publishers, 1996.

[16] Buckingham, Marcus and Curt Coffman. "First, Break All the Rules," Simon & Schuster Audio 2003.

[17] Herzberg, Frederick. "One More Time: How Do You Motivate Employees?" *Harvard Business Review.* Jan. 2003: 3 – 11.

[18] What Your Disaffected Workers Cost." *Gallup Management Journal.* 15 Mar. 2001. 15 July 2005 <http://gmj.gallup.com/content/ default.asp?ci=439>.

[19] Johnson, Steven. *Mind Wide Open.* New York: Scribner, 2004.

[20] Johnson, D.W., Skon, L., and Johnson, R. "Effects of Cooperative, Competitive, and Individualistic Conditions on Children's Problem-Solving Performance." *American Education Research Journal* 17 (1980): 83 - 93.

[21] A Balanced Scorecard is a strategic management and progress tracking methodology first developed at the Harvard Business School. See: Kaplan, R. S. and D. P. Norton. *The Balanced Scorecard: Translating Strategy into Action.* Cambridge: Harvard Business School Press, 1996.

[22] Hattie, John, and Richard Jaeger. "Assessment and Classroom learning: A deductive approach." *Assessment in Education: Principles, Policy &   Practice* 5.1 (1998): 111- 23.

[23] Prensky, Marc. *Digital Game-Based Learning.* New York: McGraw-Hill, 2001.

3

PART THREE:

WHAT REALLY MAKES SIMULATIONS WORK?

"We worked hard to build the best simulation—it was really great. The day we released the simulation, we thought we would have a huge turn-out. Instead, about eight mis-informed, very nervous individuals showed up. To top it off, when the simulation began it became apparent our facilitators were not prepared. Our simulation was great, but I guess that did not matter since we did such a poor job on everything else."

- Telecommunications executive

3.1 MARKETING AND SELLING SIMULATIONS INTERNALLY

Ralph Waldo Emerson once said, "If you build a better mouse trap, the world will beat a path to your door." In other words, if you come up with a better way to do something that needs to be done, you don't need to market it; people will come looking for you.

Emerson didn't tell the whole story, though. In fact, when it comes to simulations, his business theory was completely wrong.

At this point in the book, we hope you have discovered that simulations are a better "mousetrap" in many training situations. If you have a problem that requires an experiential learning solution, a simulation often is the fastest and most effective route to take.

But many seasoned entrepreneurs have learned the hard way that even if they have the best product around, they have nothing of real value if no one knows about it. In the best of situations, we cannot assume that a great simulation will sell itself. Like any successful product, a simulation requires a thoughtful approach to marketing.

Marketing vs. Selling: What's the Difference?

The American Marketing Association, a national non-profit organization for marketing professionals headquartered in Chicago, IL, defines *marketing* as an organizational function and set of processes for creating, communicating, and delivering value to customers and managing customer relationships in ways that benefit the organization and its stakeholders.

Selling is a subset of marketing that deals with developing, managing, and growing the customer relationship.

Marketing and selling are different, but they depend on each other for success.

When presenting simulations as the answer to your company's needs, it will be tempting to assume that the many departmental stakeholders will understand and appreciate the value of experiential learning. However, virtually all organizations struggle with different priorities competing for resources, especially budget and employee time. Company representatives responsible for allocating these resources have a variety of agendas that may not appear to immediately correspond to what a simulation will offer.

As we have seen, simulations are a relatively new solution in the training field. For the uninitiated, misperceptions are more common than facts when it comes to understanding what simulations are and what they are capable of doing. Even though simulations are often superior to traditional training methods, they can seem no different than any new program and will require internal marketing to convince decision makers to give them a chance.

You may discover that some leaders in your organization don't recognize the added value of a full business simulation, because they assume that they already have "simulations" in place. Perhaps your current training programs use role plays and other types of experiential learning. These individuals need to be educated about the differences between simulations and other forms of experiential learning, and then adequately prepared so that they know what to expect from a new simulation.

Marketing a simulation internally will also enable you to manage expectations regarding what a simulation can and cannot accomplish. Good marketing should get people realistically excited.

Your internal marketing plan for a simulation will serve two purposes. First, you will educate your stakeholders and create buy-in from management, which may be required to get a simulation adopted in the first place.

> **Lesson Learned**
>
> "When the idea of a sales simulation was introduced to me, I thought, 'Here goes the training department with a new angle to justify charging back against my budget.'"
> —VP of Marketing, telecommunications company

Second, you can use the process to educate, motivate, and excite learners. This isn't just another training proposal; this is something different, challenging, exciting, and maybe even scary. If you get participants interested and emotionally involved in the process, they'll arrive on the first day of the simulation eager to see what all the fuss is about. That's what good simulation marketing does.

> **Love-Hate Relationship**
>
> When marketing a simulation to learners, keep in mind that a love-hate perception will begin to surface.
>
> It's rare to find anyone who does not believe that learning-by-doing is the best way to acquire a new skill, and most learners will agree that simulations are a great and fun way to learn.
>
> On the flip side, when learners are asked to actually go through a simulation, the hate perception can enter the picture. Employees love the idea of a simulation, but often hate the idea of going through one.
>
> Why this paradox? Psychologists would categorize it as an approach-avoidance issue (or cognitive dissonance). People may be drawn to simulations because they are new and may help them to better their skills. However, they may worry that a simulation will make them look stupid and demonstrate to others that they don't know everything.
>
> Be aware of this issue and address it in your marketing materials; you're likely to be far more successful in

positioning your simulation with workers—especially with first-time simulation participants.

Develop and Execute an Effective Communication Plan

A communication plan should be part of the overarching branding strategy of every simulation project, internally directed to the specific business unit (or units) at the operations level.

A comprehensive communication plan provides a strong foundation for project success and establishes a structured means for tracking progress, informing participants, and motivating them to contribute to the ongoing success and of the simulation—from the pilot to the rollout to measurement and follow-up activities.

Your communication plan should include the following:

- **Simulation purpose**

  Example: To provide employees with practical experience using the company's Product Development Life Cycle (PDLC) process.

- **Communication objectives**

  Example: To ensure that managers and front-line employees fully understand the PDLC process.

  Example: To create confidence among the global PDLC teams that they'll be able to achieve the company's goals to release X number of products over the next five years.

  Example: To position the company as a progressive and innovative organization that seeks to equip its employees with the skills, knowledge, and attitudes to beat the competition.

- **Situation analysis**

  Example: Future corporate plans include expansion into Asia and further acquisition of businesses in Europe. Forecasts show that by 2007 up to fifty percent of current middle- and upper-management personnel could be serving the company in some capacity outside of the United States. In order to prepare for this, the new learning solution will collapse the learning curve and eliminate cultural confusion. This learning solution will be a real-world, highly interactive simulation to train managers and front-line employees on the new PDLC process. The simulation will place managers in situations in which they must deal with the cultural, entrepreneurial, and business challenges they will face.

Example. New competitors have entered our market space, seeking to earn a portion of our market share. In the past, our sales strategy was to take orders when customers called. The new market reality demands that we engage our customers and prospects using a consultative selling approach. Our account managers must become business consultants to their customers, making the purchase of our products and services productive and profitable. Therefore, we will implement a consultative sales simulation to re-train our sales managers and account managers, changing their mindset about their relationships to the customers and the realities they face in the new marketplace.

In addition to the items listed above, the communication plan should also include milestones, a timeline, and a list of various smaller marketing campaigns.

Internal Branding of Simulations

What is branding? Generally, a *brand* is an identifiable symbol or symbols representing an entity that makes specific promises of value.

The purpose of branding is to more efficiently sell more products or services. This is accomplished through names, logos, positioning, brand associations, and brand personality that draw customers to a product. A brand is the image of a product, line, or service, which in the mind of the consumer should be associated with quality, timeliness, reliability, and other desirable characteristics.

But branding is not just used with consumer products. The same methods and practices can be used by a training and development person who wants to market learning and development products internally.

Branding is especially important when a new or different learning solution, such as a simulation, is introduced to key decision makers. When the rollout of a simulation and any related initiatives take place over relatively long periods of time, branding can help foster recognition among stakeholders and participants of a simulation's ongoing connection to overall corporate goals and objectives.

Consider these benefits when considering the creation of your brand. A brand:

- Shapes the expectations of stakeholders
- Creates trust and emotional attachment to the success of the simulation initiative
- Makes it easier for the organization and individual learners to commit to the simulation
- Communicates a strong, consistent message about the value of intense learning experiences
- Demonstrates that the training department understands the overall business strategy and is serious about developing employees with a long-term perspective
- Helps build internal creditability
- Articulates the values that the company and department have regarding employee development

When branding a simulation for your internal marketplace, consider the following:

- Are you going to develop a signature look and feel for all marketing materials related to the simulation?

- What message do you want the simulation branding to send? What kind of image do you want to create?

- Do you want to create a simulation logo and colors that set it apart from other initiatives, or make it part of a larger corporate strategy initiative?

- Would it be advantageous to tap into an existing or complementary brand that your company is already using? Should you incorporate parts of other brand or company logos into your simulation symbols?

- Do you want to position the simulation as an exclusive experience—one for which participants are selected and in which it is a privilege to participate?

- Do you want the simulation to be perceived as challenging or fun?

Working the Power Base

However you decide to brand the simulation program, your learning program will benefit and gain acceptance faster and better if you understand the people in your organization and the supply chain as a whole. This power base of support includes the key decision makers in your organization.

Your first step in working this power base will be to understand who your supporters and detractors are.

Power is the potential to influence, either through one's title or through the respect and esteem people have for a person's knowledge, expertise, and perceived commitment. In their pivotal book *The Management of Organizational Behavior*, Hersey, Blanchard, and Johnson examine power in business. They conclude that understanding power and knowing how to use it to your advantage are just as important as actually attaining power on paper.[24]

Power shifts according to situation. Understanding and working the informal and formal power system when introducing a simulation in your organization can go a long way toward helping you to gain acceptance for simulations as an important component of the performance development process.

As you determine how to approach and talk to others about a simulation and potentially enlist their help, here are some important considerations.

In your marketing materials and during face-to-face communications, are you:

- Emphasizing the simulation's fit with your company's corporate vision and strategy, technology, and/or financial plan?
- Broadcasting testimonials and sponsorship endorsements from highly influential individuals? These endorsements are most influential when they come from high-ranking managers who enjoy the esteem of other managers and employees.
- Building your presentation based on the existing business?
- Making recommendations that are workable given existing resources? If not, what is the plan for adding additional resources?
- Taking into consideration the need for additional technology to support the simulation? Is your IT department on board?

In your presentation of the simulation, are you:

- Making the recommendation tangible by painting a picture?
- Articulating the benefits without over-selling?
- Connecting the relevant features, advantages, and benefits of simulations to your audience?

Working with Stakeholders

The best way to understand stakeholders' needs is to consider the situation from their mindset. To do this, ask yourself, "What keeps them awake at night?"

Perhaps your executive stakeholders are concerned with the decisions that their managers are making. Or perhaps they wonder whether employees truly understand the impact that their decisions and actions have on the business. Whatever it may be, your success lies in recognizing and speaking to those needs.

Approaching people within the organization

The classic *diffusion of innovation model*, a long-time standard in marketing circles for understanding how ideas spread, can be a useful tool when approaching your stakeholders to gain support for a simulation initiative.

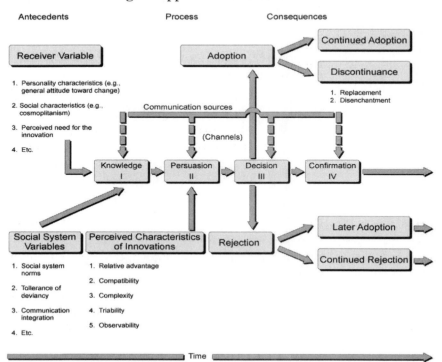

The diffusion of innovation model divides people into five categories: innovators, early adaptors, early majority, late majority and laggards. As you can see in the diagram, these categories traditionally follow a bell-shaped curve.

One way to speed the adoption of an innovation (in this case, the simulation) is to make a conscious effort to identify, gain the support of, and work with opinion leaders within the organization. Opinion leaders are those people in or associated with your organization who can influence others on a regular basis. These are the people who will best serve as champions for your project.

Finding a champion is not a solution by itself. Finding the *right* champion, however, will help you make significant progress toward success. There often are people in organizations whose support will bring a negative impact from other, more influential stakeholders in the company; identify these negative influencers early and consider the ways your potential champions are viewed throughout the organization before asking them to participate.

Here are some questions to consider when finding the right champion:

- Who are the decision makers in the company? How can you effectively pitch an idea to them?

- Do the innovators in your organization have influence potential with others, or are they considered out of touch with the real world, lacking urgency or focus, or even flaky? (This is often the case with research and development or academic types.)

- How is your department viewed? If your group consists of those who have been innovators in the past, how have the innovations worked? What were the results?

- If you are going to test a pilot simulation, who should you ask to participate? Who will understand the innovations you are introducing and help you to create both a formal and informal network of positive buzz?

Be sure to help your champions by giving them the information and tools that they need. Provide easy-to-use professional aids to help them move the message out to the rest of the company and tell a story that will compel others to buy into the simulation.

Ultimately, the opinion leaders of your organization should become your champions. Finding champions that support your vision will help spread the message, which will speed up the diffusion of the simulation.

3.2 ENSURING THE SIMULATION DOES WHAT IT IS SUPPOSED TO DO

Before releasing a new simulation to the full targeted area of your organization, conduct a pre-release well in advance of your launch date. A *pre-release* is a test run designed to ensure that everything is running smoothly; it will allow you to fix any embarrassing problems prior to the general implementation of the learning program.

In a pre-release, run the simulation with a small, select group of participants. Organize the program before, during, and after the simulation exactly the way you expect to in the general release. Test everything: all communications, instructions, debriefs, assessments, and, of course, the simulation itself.

The following simulation pre-release checklist will help ensure that your simulation did what it was suppose to do during the pre-release: improve participant performance in order to achieve the business goal.

Simulation Pre-Release Checklist

	Questions
Motivation	• Were the participants motivated? Were they engaged emotionally during the simulation? • What was their motivation level before vs. after the simulation? • Are they going to share their exciting, useful experience with others, or are they going to tell others that it was a dull experience of little use?

	Questions
Realism	<ul><li>Did the simulation create an environment similar to what one would expect in the real world?</li><li>Was the content realistic?</li><li>Were the tasks or activities realistic?</li><li>Did the participants leave saying that the simulation was applicable to their job, or did they feel that it was hard to suspend their disbelief?</li></ul>
Application	<ul><li>Could the skills practiced in the simulation be applied to participants' jobs?</li><li>Did the participants leave feeling that they could immediately apply the skills to their jobs?</li></ul>
Function	<ul><li>Did the simulation function correctly?</li><li>Did all the technology elements do what they were designed to do?</li><li>If evaluation engines where used, did they accept inputs and generate correct outputs?</li><li>Were the tools easy to use, or did participants require a lot of coaching?</li><li>Did the participants feel that the simulation worked, or did they feel like "testers?"</li></ul>

	Questions
Engagement	• Was the emotional throttle set correctly? • Were participants too stressed? • Were they bored? • What was their energy level while working in teams or participating in debriefing sessions?
Environment	• Did the storyline hold together? • Were the goals clear? • Did the participants achieve the goals? • Was the feedback beneficial to the participants? • Did the rounds or levels of the simulation flow? • Did the participants need a lot of guidance, or were they able to understand what to do?
Content	• What content, if any, was missing before, during, or after the simulation? • Was too much detail provided, or not enough? • Did the supporting materials provide enough background information for both novice and experienced participants?

	Questions
Technology	• Was the right technology used? • Did the participants spend too much time tinkering with or learning to use the technology or figuring out what to do?
Performance	• Did the participants achieve the desired performance level? • Did participants demonstrate the targeted skill and knowledge during the simulation? • What on-the-job reinforcements after the simulation would ensure transfer of their learning to the workplace?
Experience	• What was the overall experience like, from the participant's perspective? • Was it memorable? • Do participants see value in simulations?

3.3 FACILITATORS

Even the best-designed simulation can be a terrible experience for everyone involved if the facilitators aren't capable. Facilitators are the glue that holds the simulation experience together, so it is especially important to select talented individuals.

Qualities of a Great Facilitator

Be sure that your simulation facilitator is capable of dealing with ambiguity. Most business simulations are not linear or predictable, meaning that no matter how many times a facilitator guides learners through a simulation, new situations and problems will arise. For every issue encountered, there are a number of different ways to respond. A good facilitator realizes that there is no "right" or "wrong" answer and is comfortable working in such an environment.

A good facilitator also is good at Socratic questioning. He or she can design questions that will help learners unlock and understand the knowledge that the simulation presents. This gives the learners a chance to discover lessons without feeling lectured.

Effective facilitators are able to understand and work within a complex business model. Advanced simulations demonstrate the impact of decisions across many different business functions and units. Facilitators must grasp these concepts and feel comfortable with systems and critical thinking, understanding how parts of a business impact and interact both with one another and with the business as a whole. Just because there is a problem in one area of a simulated business, for example, doesn't necessarily mean that the cause of the problem can be found in that same area. A facilitator who can work through this type of thinking will be able to guide participants to similar discoveries.

A good facilitator has a strong business background and working knowledge of various business disciplines. Few businesspeople are experts in all disciplines. However, a good facilitator has a working knowledge of key principles from the many disciplines involved in the simulation.

Finally, a good facilitator possesses vast amounts of patience. New facilitators sometimes believe that they need to give learners answers immediately, especially when learners are frustrated. However, participants need time and space to discover and learn concepts on their own. Simulations are designed so that simple answers are not always necessary or desirable. A facilitator needs to know when to jump in and help someone and when to allow a learner to figure things out for herself.

Training a Facilitator

It can be difficult to find someone who embodies all of the characteristics of an effective facilitator. The good news is that you can train a facilitator.

Before the specific simulation training begins, potential facilitators should already possess a broad knowledge of the company as a whole. Once they have that, the best way to prepare them for the simulation is to allow them time to experience the simulation themselves and play it through several times. They will become personally familiar with the situations and emotions that arise during the training process and will familiarize themselves with how to deal with them.

If possible, facilitators-in-training also should be offered an opportunity to talk to the teams who designed the simulation (programmers, writers, business experts, etc.). This will allow them to garner "behind the scenes" knowledge of why the simulation contains certain aspects.

You might also require your facilitators to interview or observe other, more seasoned facilitators to learn more about the "human" aspect of simulations—those aspects of the experience that will not be found in any book. Specifically, what are the best ways to handle learners in certain situations? Ideally, facilitators should sit in on a simulation class conducted by an experienced facilitator.

Another tip for improving trainees' facilitation skills is to require that facilitators create in advance a list of questions to ask after each round. These questions should be generic enough to be used repeatedly, but specific enough to facilitate the learning process. Questions can be borrowed from other facilitators or developed in teams, depending upon how comfortable the facilitator is with question creation. A number of sample questions will be provided in the debriefing section later in this section. However, we recommend that each facilitator creates his own questions, because in the process, he will learn more about the simulation.

A facilitator training to join an existing simulation program may also choose to enlist the help of learners from previous simulations. In most training programs, one team in every class will truly excel within a simulation. If a facilitator finds herself stumped over an issue, previous top performers can provide an external perspective and insights to solve the problem. Some may disagree with this advice and argue that seeking help from participants degrades the facilitator in the eyes of trainees, but it often can have the opposite effect. When an individual is willing to admit his shortcomings, learners often appreciate the fact that the person is not trying to serve as a "lecturer" or "teacher," but as a facilitator whose primary goal is to help them succeed. This can lead to tight-knit, supportive environments where learners feel less leery of seeking help and guidance from others.

Facilitator Influence on the Emotional Throttle

A strong facilitator is aware of the emotional state of her group of learners at all times during a simulation. This is especially important in situations where learners are likely to experience strong emotions, ranging from anger and excitement to disappointment and elation.

If participant emotions hit extreme levels during a simulation, the learning process may be hindered not just for one individual but for the entire class.

For example, a participant may feel that he has made so many mistakes that he chooses to stop taking the simulation seriously. If this participant no longer feels emotionally invested in the simulation, things can become rapidly worse for the entire group. He will begin to make choices at random, won't learn anything, and, chances are, will distract those around him. The worst-case scenario is the frustrated, embarrassed learner who counterattacks the simulation as invalid, inappropriate, or otherwise not worthwhile.

Such a negative attitude can poison a group and damage the reputation of the simulation. The troublemaker's attitude and actions will affect those around him—so much so that others in the group will also stop taking the simulation seriously. Suddenly, the facilitator is faced with a room of people who are off task, wasting time, and not learning a thing. While this may sound extreme, one person can and sometimes does lead the group astray.

A talented facilitator can prevent this situation from escalating by observing her participants and stepping in to intervene with the frustrated learner immediately. If the facilitator decides that someone is struggling to the point of giving up, she should offer help in the form of hints and encouragement, and most importantly help them help themselves.

Preparing Facilitators to Deal with Interpersonal Team Issues

Because business simulations often require learners to work in groups, an array of issues can arise among members of a team.

One team in a simulation project might have great chemistry, while another team experiences interpersonal conflicts that escalate to mutual dislike, even hatred. A team may consist entirely of individuals motivated to get things done and pitch in where necessary, or a team might have one or more lazy members who won't pull their weight. Equally disruptive are individuals who brashly take charge, issuing orders in inappropriate, even disrespectful manners to their peers.

There is no way to predict what will happen within particular teams. The dynamics are the same as they are in the real world, where people often struggle to work together. The simulation facilitator's role is not to stop conflict, but to be aware of situations and coach teams through the difficulties.

Here are some team-related warning signs that facilitators should look for and respond to quickly when needed:

Someone wants to fire someone else. This can happen for a variety of reasons. Perhaps one person isn't putting in as much effort as other people on the team. Perhaps two team members' personalities simply clash. Or perhaps one team member isn't grasping the complexity of the simulation as quickly as the rest of the team. Facilitator reactions to such issues can and should vary depending on the underlying root of the problem and the team's level of unhappiness over the situation.

A facilitator should refrain from trying to fix the problem. Remember, team dynamics are a critical part of any business. Therefore, a facilitator should challenge the team to think through similar issues they've experienced in their careers and work together to come up with a solution. Often, a brief break from the simulation to focus on teambuilding results in a stronger team.

Having said that, some personalities will clash no matter what a facilitator does, and some participants bring conflict from other parts of their work life into the simulation. If the dislike between members is so great that it disrupts their learning experience (as well as that of their other team members), it might be best to move the problem participant to another team.

Someone does not participate. This often occurs when a participant enters the learning situation without interest or motivation. If a learner slacks off, the facilitator should remind her that her evaluation or grade is tied to the rest of the team. In other words, her failure to perform won't just hurt her; it will hurt everyone with whom she is working. Often peer pressure from teammates addresses this situation quickly and effectively.

There are circumstances in which a person does not participate because she has not developed the foundational skills or knowledge needed within the simulation. If the facilitator identifies this challenge in one of the participants, his first task is to determine if the individual can gain the skills and knowledge before the next round of the simulation. An alternative solution would be for teams to work together to identify where individual talents can be best utilized.

Simulations are so broad that there is almost always a great fit for everyone somewhere. This is a critical real-world skill, and facilitators need to find a way to match talents to the different tasks within the simulation.

If a facilitator experiences a participant arrogantly acting as if she has all the answers, the facilitator should stress that part of the simulation experience is learning to collaborate and listen to other people's ideas.

Competition gets out of hand. How does a facilitator deal with the competitive aspect of a simulation? By its very nature, a simulation evokes a sense of competition among its participants both in the desire to win and in the tendency to pursue short-term wins.

Some people will do anything to win. Whether the simulation is based on competition or not, or whether the work is done individually or in teams, facilitators will face learners who cannot seem to stand finishing even second. Some level of competitive drive from simulation participants creates focus and improves learning in ways similar to what people experience in the real world. However, competition taken to an extreme can emotionally intimidate or shut participants down, hindering the learning of the team.

The point of a simulation is to become an environment where learners feel safe to learn by doing, making mistakes along the way without fear of retribution. Before letting the competition escalate to a level where it does not add value to the learning environment or where team members must be removed, the facilitator should adjust the competitive level. The types, amounts, and the way in which feedback and information is provided to the participants can be used to control competitiveness. For example, the facilitator may elect not to share competing team scores or results.

This is one of the key reasons why feedback in a simulation should not be solely dependent on the automatic model of the simulation; if facilitators do not feel that they can adjust competitive levels, they should let the simulation designers know about the problem and request appropriate adjustments.

"Gaming" a Simulation

Facilitators should be aware that learners may try to "game" a simulation in order to work around the lessons.

Gaming involves studying and trying to understand the simulation model and program in order to submit answers that the system will reward, rather than using business skills to make correct choices and doing the hard work that a simulation requires. In simple simulations, this is fairly easy for learners to do—but they will suffer as a result when they return to real jobs in the real world. They may have great scores and perform wonderfully on paper, but these learners will have learned nothing except how to beat the simulation.

Gaming is almost impossible to do with more advanced, responsive simulations that change randomly according to learners' decisions and input.

The best way to prevent gaming is to announce to each class that the simulation cannot be gamed, but that if learners try to do so, their overall performance review will suffer. Even if this is not the case, and the simulation *can* be gamed, it will still deter a great percentage of learners from trying.

Performance and learning

A person who performs poorly during a simulation may actually be learning more than anyone else in the room.

Consider this example:

Jim has a business background, and Bob has an accounting background. Both are of the same intelligence level, and both participate in a business simulation.

Jim performs significantly better then Bob. Why? Jim's background gave him an advantage. He already possessed knowledge about how to run a business. While Bob is good at financial matters, he did not have the overall knowledge necessary to make good business decisions.

Just because Jim performed better then Bob, however, does not mean that Jim learned more. If Jim already had knowledge in the areas covered by the simulation, he was simply drawing from his former experiences -- not necessarily assimilating the skills the simulation sought to teach.

Bob, by contrast, did not have any previous knowledge from which to draw. He failed to perform as well as Jim, but he learned more, because he was forced to concentrate throughout the simulation, making many mistakes along the way. Jim, on the other hand, "glided" through the simulation without picking up many new skills.

Understanding the difference will help a facilitator be more effective at providing feedback. Additionally, if a facilitator observes someone gliding through the simulation, she can change that person's role in the simulation. For example, Jim could become a coach or step into another role that may be completely outside his skill or knowledge level.

Don't Forget to Debrief

Debriefing an individual learner or an entire training class is an important process that generally occurs after a simulation is complete.

Facilitators debrief their classes for a number of reasons. First, facilitators answer any questions that participants might have and ensure that they understood the process that they just underwent. Second, debriefing serves to summarize and process the participants' new knowledge and skills. Doing so helps to cement the newly acquired materials in learners' brains, thereby raising retention rates.

There are many ways to conduct a successful debriefing exercise. Facilitators can arrange for a conversation among learners, allowing them to discuss their experiences. Alternately, the facilitator can create and provide a questionnaire that covers the various learning objectives taught throughout the simulation. Each learner may be asked to give a presentation summarizing her experiences, followed by a Q&A session.

All debriefings, regardless of style, should address several core issues. The following questions have been adapted from an article written by Fritzsche, Leonard, Boscia and Anderson called the Simulation Debriefing Procedures:[25]

- **Personal reactions:** General questions meant to start the conversation.

Questions: How are you feeling after this experience? What emotions did you go through during the simulation? What did you like most? What did you like least? Was this activity worthwhile? Why or why not?

- **Discussion of Events:** Gives learners a chance to share what they experienced (depending on the type of simulation, everyone might have gone through the same events or encountered different ones).

Questions: Which events from the simulation stand out most in your memory? What were the main events? Did your long-term and short-term decision-making have different effects? Why or why not? Which events proved pivotal to the outcome of the simulation for you/your team?

- **Discussion of problems:** Opportunity to address specific problems that participants encountered during the simulation and hear about problems that others encountered, as well. By doing so, they will learn not only how to solve the problems they encountered, but how to address problems that they have yet to face.

Questions: Did anyone encounter any interesting problems that they overcame or problems that they couldn't solve? How did you deal with the problems that arose? Were these problems similar to those you have encountered or will encounter in real life? Why or why not? Would you solve them the same way in real life? Why or why not? What was the biggest "ah-ha" learning experience you had that led to a solution?

- **Intended learning outcomes:** Prompts learners to analyze themselves and their learning.

Questions: Did you learn anything new? Why or why not? Did you use old skills in new ways? How did you use these old skills? What was it about the simulation that caused such learning to take place?

- **Links to the real world:** Ties all of the experiences encountered and lessons and skills learned in the simulation to reality. It also ensures that learners make connections between what they learned in the simulation and its application to the real world.

  Questions: How is what you experienced in the simulation tied to the real world? How did your decisions affect the whole company? Do you think that you will encounter the same situations in reality? Would you make the same decisions in real life? Why or why not?

- **Ethical issues:** A chance to discuss any ethical problems that participants encountered during the simulation.

  Questions: Did you face any ethical temptations during the simulation? Why or why not? What ethical problems did you face? How did you handle them? Do you think you would encounter the same problems in real life? Would you handle them in the same way or differently?

- **Company-specific:** Gives the learners a chance to tie what they learned to their specific jobs.

  Questions: How is what you experienced in the simulation tied to your job? Will you approach decisions different now that you have been through the simulation? What will you stop doing or start doing in your job?

The debriefing process does not need to be tedious or formal. Indeed, some of the best debriefing experiences are freely-flowing discussions that create an engaging experience just like simulation learning itself.

This time should be focused on helping learners reflect on what they learned. By doing so, simulation experiences are reinforced and given a longer "shelf life." Even if they aren't used right away, the skills learned within a simulation will stay with learners until they are needed.

3.4 IT'S NOT OVER: CAPTURE, EVALUATE, MEASURE, IMPROVE

After the successful or not-so-successful release of a business simulation training program, many companies make the mistake of not looking back and failing to improve on what they started.

Immediately after the simulation, the training team responsible for the program should capture what worked and what did not, measure the impact, evaluate the issues and data, and create a plan to improve the overall experience of the simulation.

This is the best time for honesty. How was the communication before, during, and after the simulation? Were the learners motivated and engaged? Did they learn what the simulation intended for them to learn? Do the learners feel they can apply their new skills to their job?

Capture

Simulations that take employees out of their normal routines often create an informal buzz of chatter and opinions. Sometimes that buzz can be quite loud. Participants talk about the emotional experience and compare stories long after the event has ended. These stories can work to your advantage and help you in the same way Academy Award nominations help movie studios increase interest in their films.

After the simulation, be ready with recording equipment and a pen. Capture testimonials—both good and bad. Use the good to extend your communication plan. Use the bad to help you improve the simulation.

Be sure you truly understand the difference between good and bad feedback. After a simulation, you'll want to hear great praise for the awesome learning experience you just provided. Remember, though, that participants' emotions are also high. What may sound like criticism or a flaw in the simulation is actually a huge opportunity for future success. Honest criticism from participants is golden if you can see through your emotional reactions and find the pathway to improvement. The same criticism or complaint from many different teams and people may indicate a basic design flaw in the simulation. Test it against the design and determine if the design achieved its goal.

In addition to debriefing, use questionnaires to survey participants' managers (which will also encourage managers to play the crucial role of post-simulation on-the-job reinforcement). Check for changes in key workplace performance indicators, such as sales results, customer satisfaction scores, process metric improvement, or any other business measure that the simulation should have impacted.

Evaluate

In the Olympics, the difference between a gold medal and no medal at all can often be measured by a tenth of a second, and sometimes mere hundredths of a second.

With so much at stake and with so little room for error, it's no wonder that professional athletes constantly measure their performance in training. The benchmarks of time, distance, strength, and speed help athletes understand their current performance compared to other athletes in their sport. Their measurements help them recognize any gaps in their performance.

Smart businesses also measure their performance against benchmark standards. Executives may analyze current and desired performance areas in order to generate a list of priorities and identify gaps in company performance. For example, a manufacturing company that wishes to become the market-share leader in its industry will measure its current performance against the level it wishes to achieve. To quantify its current performance, the company may look at current sales, market share, marketing efforts, customer service, distribution, and overall operations. All this information helps a company to better understand where it is and where it needs to go.

Once your company understands what your gaps are and what your desired performance level (or goal) should be, you will be better prepared to create or buy a simulation that will focus on improving performance and achieving your specific goals.

Measure

More than fifty years ago, Donald Kirkpatrick described four levels of evaluating a learning experience:[26]

- Reaction–how did learners perceive the experience?
- Learning–did participants acquire the targeted skills and knowledge?
- Behavioral–did this learning change their behavior in the workplace?
- Impact–did it change the performance of their organization for the better?

We have already addressed the critical factors to consider in the *reaction* and *learning* levels.

Gauging *behavioral* workplace changes after a simulation training experience requires engaging the participants' managers through surveys and other methods outlined above. Involving managers and helping them to observe changes in performance will benefit your simulation training program in two ways. First, manager support and feedback provides evidence of the effectiveness or ineffectiveness of the simulation. Second, it engages managers in reinforcing new skills and knowledge so that they become ingrained, consistent, and long-term.

Kirkpatrick's final level of evaluation—measuring *impact* of the simulation on the original strategy—brings the simulation review full circle to its original purpose.

Thousands of organizations and companies—including for-profit, not-for-profit, and government agencies—have adopted the Balanced Scorecard or one of its many imitators. How your company measures the success of your strategy does not matter as much as the fact that you are seeking to measure it at all. Businesses in different industries focus on various high-level measures to see if they are executing their strategy. Some use financial measures, like revenue growth, operating profit, stock price, EBITDA, or profitability by customer relationship. Others use market metrics: market share, market rank/position, or market perception of the company and it products or services.

Whatever key metrics your organization uses, be sure to tie your simulation results to movement in these specific numbers. Line managers and executives find this kind of impact measurement the most credible and the most important.

Improve

It's not enough to simply collect information; you have to use what you have learned in order to create a better learning environment for future participants. From all of these sources of evaluative data, you and your company will glean intelligence that will help you improve future simulation rounds and projects.

More important, your team can use your experiences to improve the degree to which learners change their behaviors in the workplace, which will result in the greatest overall performance impact on the organization. Ultimately, simulations attract so much attention because of the effects they have on the execution of strategy.

3.5 THE ELEMENTS OF A SIMULATION

What makes a simulation a simulation? Are role play games simulations? What about an excel spreadsheet that has a clearly defined goal, provides feedback and guides the learner through a serious of 'what if' exercise? Or, does a simulation need to include various emotional, real-world issues?

In Part Two of this book, we covered the various design and decision points in detail. This section takes our evaluation one step further, providing a brief checklist of the primary elements most often used to build simulations.

These are the elements of high-impact business simulations. Not all of these elements need to present in every simulation; some simple simulations might only have two or three of the elements. Those simulations can be useful on a limited scale, but a high-impact business simulation—one that fully engages the learner—requires all of these elements.

Filtering– There's no doubt that we live in the information age. Today, even the simplest decisions require us to process huge quantities of information. Almost every businessperson faces situations where they feel overwhelmed with information. A crucial skill for success in any business is to learn to filter the information, eliminating the noise and taking advantage of what's important.

A simulation must develop a learner's ability to use information wisely. That's the real world. As with any of the elements the details, like how many sources and types of information to incorporate may vary, but a high-impact business simulation must require learners to filter a great deal of information in order to make their decisions.

179

Interruptions–Interruptions are a regular part of the real world, and they're an integral part of a high-impact simulation. Learners should encounter regular interruptions, things that distract them from the task at hand and force them to focus 100% on something else.

In the real world, interruptions take many forms, including urgent phone calls, e-mails, or "drop ins" from co-workers. Simulations can use all of these and others to force learners to spread their focus between tasks and prioritize activities.

Goals–Business people are goal oriented. Research shows that people with clearly-defined goals tend to earn three to five thousand dollars more a month, are healthier, and live a more balanced life. Goals provide motivation, direction, and reward.

A high-impact business simulation must have clearly defined goals, both for the individual learners and for the entire simulation. A defined goal is a clearly obtainable target that the learner tries to hit or exceed, such as a sales target, market share, or safety rating. To become fully engaged in the simulation, it's important the learner can define and track personal goals in addition to the ones being tracked by the simulation.

Feedback–Most of us receive feedback every hour of every day. In the business world, feedback comes in many different flavors and is crucial for success, allowing us to accurately evaluate ourselves and make changes when we need to. Yet most training programs provide very little direct or indirect feedback.

Feedback is a crucial part of a high-impact business simulation, because it challenges the learner to examine the cause-and-effect of their decisions and expands a employee's ability to solve complex problems. Learning how to evaluate and react to feedback is a critical business skill. Incorporating several feedback elements accelerates the learning and guides the learner to an expected performance target.

Exploration–One of the problems with the real world is that we can only make one decision at a time. We might like the chance to try out different options, but by the time the results of a decision are obvious it's usually too late to try something else. This had led to the popularity of "what if" questions, often an exercise in futility in the real world but simulations are different.

One of the most important elements of a high-impact simulation is its ability to allow a leaner to ask and answer "what if" questions. In an effective simulation learners are able to explore different options and observe how the business might react.

Collaboration–According to Carl Larson, author of *Team Excellence* and *What Makes Team Work*, cooperative learning is one of the most effective tools of accelerated learning. When people collaborate in teams they learn more and more quickly than they ever would working alone. In addition to giving learners the chance to discuss questions and problems, collaboration allows learners to get a new perspective and develop important real-world communication.

High-impact business simulations must include elements of collaboration and teamwork. Even if learners work primarily on their own, there should be an opportunity to collaborate with other learners in discussion groups, debriefs, or checkpoints.

Tension–Information and events are not linear. Work and interactions are not neat and predictable. We are constantly filtering various inputs and reacting to situations. All of these factors add tension to the real world, and they explain why tension is a key part of effective simulations.

Incorporating tension into a simulation increases learner engagement and deepens the learning experience. A healthy level of tension heightens our ability to learn.

Gaming–From the time we're children almost all of us would rather be playing a game than sitting in a classroom.

The same is true when we're adults. In simulations gaming elements provide motivation, structure, and a goal, they also create a competitive environment for learning.

A business simulation can include gaming elements without becoming a game. Including gaming elements, like scorekeeping, competition, and surprise variables can increase the entertainment value and fun of a simulation.

Acceleration–Wouldn't it be great if you could fast forward the clock a few months or years ahead and evaluate the impact your decision had on the business before you actually made it? That is exactly what a high-impact business simulation does. Within a simulation, the impact of time is played out so learners may gain valuable insights to the effects of their decisions.

Coach–A good coach doesn't just tell you what to do; she helps you discover success on your own. The role of a simulation coach is to get the learners to question themselves, their ideas, theirs choices and their results.

Though there are some great self-guided simulations, a high-impact business simulation should provide opportunities for a coach or facilitator to ask Socratic questions.

Model– No matter what type of simulation (one guided by a person or one guided by technology) it must have a way to judge and direct learners. In technology-based simulations, there is usually a computational engine that mathematically evaluates learners' responses. In a facilitated or human-guided simulation, a rule book or flow diagram is used to evaluate learners' responses.

In technology-based simulations, the design and sophistication of the engine is the key to the simulation's success. A simple decision engine guides a learner down a tree of predetermined outcomes. A dynamic engine has a wider variety of possible outcomes and based on learners' responses it can produce a wide variety of results. The most powerful engine, a responsive engine, actually evaluates the quality of thinking in learners and creates unique results for each user based on their inputs and decisions. Unlike decision or dynamic engines, responsive engine driven simulations will never be the same twice; each learner has a totally unique experience.

3.6 RICHNESS AND REACH

The *richness and reach* model is intended to help you visually map learning solutions according to how engaging they are and how many participants each program is capable of teaching at any one time.

Richness refers to how interactive, engaging, and realistic you want your learning solution to be, which directly correlates to how thoroughly you need participants to *know* the information or demonstrate skill to be able to *do* the tasks that execute your strategy.

Of course, training and development is only cost-effective when it is experienced by the entire audience that needs to be reached. Thus, the **reach** portion of the model addresses how many participants the training program or course is designed to train from a *limited* scale of one person in a coaching or mentoring situation to a *global* reach in an on-line simulation.

In the richness and reach diagram, you can see the interaction of different types of learning solutions in relationship to one another. The solutions are divided into four quadrants based on the four possibilities in the richness and reach model. Quadrant I, in the lower left, depicts learning solutions with

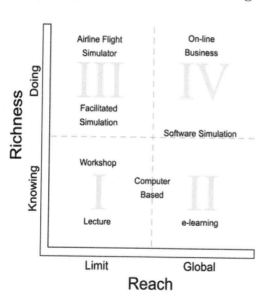

relatively low levels of richness (focused on knowing) and limited reach.

Flight simulators used to train military or commercial pilots offer one of the most engaging, challenging, and realistic simulation environments available. In many ways it's better than the real world, because participants can be put into more problematic situations in one simulator session than they might encounter in a lifetime of flying real aircraft. As shown in Quadrant III, a flight simulator has a great deal of richness (focuses on doing) but since only one or two people at one time can experience the training, it has a very limited reach.

In Quadrant II, a typical e-learning course has a global reach but often lacks the richness of a well-designed, computer-based course or a classroom workshop in which the facilitator engages the participants in various team activities and skill practice sessions. Most e-learning is designed for teaching principles, concepts, processes, and procedural information—in other words, material that is based on knowing. Software simulations, on the other hand, offer more interactions; the training would have a global reach and would fall between Quadrant II (lower right) and Quadrant IV (upper right).

Traditional classroom training has a limited reach and varies in richness from lecture to hands-on facilitated simulations. On the other hand, well-designed on-line business simulations achieve both a high level of richness and a potentially extensive reach.

Consider this model in light of your own current learning solutions. Are most of your training programs in Quadrant I? Do you have a large e-learning catalog? Are most employees gaining knowledge and skills without opportunities to practice *doing?*

The Hard Truth

Most organizational training programs fall into Quadrants I and II, teaching people what they need to know. And as we have seen, for many business purposes this is fine. However, when employees need be able do something to execute your strategy in ways that demonstrate their understanding of the business as a whole, more of your learning solutions must fall into Quadrants III and IV.

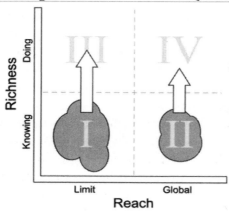

Ultimately, to save money and become more competitive, organizations will need to identify key Quadrant I and II courses and move them to Quadrant III and IV.

Most corporate training falls into Quadrant I. To reduce costs, many skills are transferred or supplemented by Quadrant II courses

Often, these doing-based experiences happen only during on-the-job training. Though this is one of the best experiential methods, we explored in Part 1 why this can be a costly undertaking, both in time and money. By plotting your organization's learning programs in the richness and reach model, your team can begin to identify ways to optimize the learning solutions budget to include some training areas that address these two quadrants.

To gain the most information from this analysis, diagram both your current programs and any future learning solutions you will implement. Be sure to prioritize your goals and list various strategies that your employees will need to execute in order to achieve these goals. This will help you be more selective when deciding which learning solutions to evolve from Quadrants I and II (knowing) into Quadrants III and IV (doing). Remember, the goal is not necessarily to replace your current learning solutions. Rather, you should leverage what is in place and find opportunities to extend key skills into the "Doing Quadrants."[27]

Typically, training departments are apprehensive about moving into these two new quadrants, believing that it is 1) too costly, and 2) too unpredictable and potentially risky. Both are valid concerns. However, it's too costly *not* to move *some* training into the Doing Quadrants.

Consider the estimated costs of repeating the same (or similar) courses year after year, plus the lost opportunities because of under-performing employees and missed goals. Invite your executives and stakeholders to do the same. In our experience, you'll find that the costs are far greater than the cost to extend an existing program.

Many corporations gravitate toward generic or traditional training courses because they are controllable (with a moderately talented design and/or facilitator). On the other hand, courses in the Doing Quadrant are unpredictable by design. Developing critical and problem-solving skills, systemic thinking, and confidence requires employees to explore and try various actions. Ultimately you want your employees approach their work with a mindset that reality is unpredictable, so like the US Marine Corps, we will "adapt, overcome, and improvise."

There are many great, cost effective, and yet powerful solutions for extending existing training courses and other learning solutions, such as Documentary Learning™, Embedded Simulations, and Action Learning. For the skills that are critical to your organization's strategic execution, a business simulation is ultimately the most cost effective and predictable solution.

---

24 Hersey, P. Blanchard, K. and Johnson, D. T. *Management of Organizational Behavior.* New Jersey: Prentice Hall, 2000.

[25] Fritzsche, Dave, Nancy Leonard, Marian W. Boscia, and Phil Anderson. "Simulation Debriefing Procedures." *Developments in Business Simulation and Experiential Learning* 31 (2004): 337 - 338.

[26] Kirkpatrick, Donald L. *Evaluating Training Programs: The Four Levels.* San Francisco: Berrett-Koehler Publishers, 1998.

[27] There are additional resources and tools available at the RLS website (www.regislearning.com) to help you develop and apply the richness and reach model to your organization, as well as cases for how to select and extend your existing training programs from the Knowing Quadrant to the Doing Quadrant.

4

PART FOUR:

CONCLUSION

An Impressive History

Using simulations to solve training problems is not a new idea. For centuries, people have used simulations for many of the same reasons we use them today; to make learning faster and more effective and to reduce the costs associated with "rookie mistakes." One of the first simulations was an early form of chess developed in India as a war simulation.[28] Young princes played to learn battle strategy and tactics. It was too costly to send soldiers into battle unprepared, but the only effective way to prepare for battle was with battle, or with the closest thing available–good battle simulations. These were the future military leaders; they needed to know how to run a battle, how to make good decisions under pressure, and how to think about many different things at once.

Hundreds of years later, the Royal Air Force used the Link flight simulator to train pilots during World War II. Again, trainees needed specialized skills that they couldn't learn in the classroom, but it would have been far too costly to send them up in real planes. Again, simulations allowed quick effective training without the same risks of real world experience.

After World War II, businesses began to explore the possibilities of simulations. The Monte Carlo analysis is one early example of businesses using models to predict and test business outcomes. The Monte Carlo analysis allowed users to model solutions to problems which were too expensive, too risky, or too complicated to be adopted in the business. This technique significantly improved researchers' abilities to predict the outcomes of situations in the real world, without the expense or risk of actually implementing many different solutions. Unlike earlier simulations like Link, however, the Monte Carlo analysis wasn't designed as a training tool, but as a modeling tool used by analysts and researchers to predict results.

The use of simulations for business training began in 1957, when the American Management Association (AMA) introduced the first business training simulation. Much like current business simulations, the early AMA simulation programs allowed teams of participants to make business decisions and receive feedback about those decisions. Within three years of the AMA program's debut, nearly one hundred similar simulations were in use in businesses all over the world.

Today businesses and business schools use simulations for many of the same reasons that Indian royalty used them hundreds of years ago; traditional training is too time-consuming or the costs of mistakes are too high. Training departments today face the same concerns that have faced trainers for years, and whether you're preparing an Indian prince for war or a retail manager to run a drugstore, simulations provide effective training without the risks of sending a rookie into the field.

A Changing Landscape

In the last five years, businesses' attitudes toward simulations have begun to change, allowing simulations to move quickly from the MBA classroom and the executive boardroom to the corporate training room.

There are many factors contributing to this trend, including expense, time, technology, change, competition and globalization. These offer valuable insights into why businesses have begun flocking to simulations as training tools like never before.

Expense–For decades, simulations have remained out of reach of all but the wealthiest organizations. In the 1980s, it was not uncommon for a full custom business simulation to cost millions of dollars, making simulations impractical as training tools. Recent technological advances and increased competition by existing and emergent simulation vendors, however, have lowered the price of custom and off-the-shelf simulations significantly.

Time–Because workplace simulations can now be created more rapidly and then quickly and easily adjusted as training needs change and arise over time, they now are more feasible as organizational training tools. Using emergent computer modeling technology, graphics programs, digital video and other twenty-first century tools, it is now possible to create business simulations in a fraction of the time it took a generation ago. Simple business simulations based on an Excel spreadsheet, for example, can be developed in a matter of days, while more complex simulations that utilize responsive modeling technology and adaptive content may take only weeks or months to create.

Changing Realities–The realities of modern business are changing: In today's business environment, keeping pace with rapid change is the challenge *du jour*. Information is growing exponentially, business decisions are more complex, team collaboration stretches across the globe, and workplace challenges are increasing–with no sign of slowing down. In a business climate that requires fewer people to do more, to learn to do it in less time, and to understand more completely how every aspect of the business works, organizations are challenged like never before to train people fast. In this environment, simulations' ability to immerse learners in fictional environments that mimic the real-world workplace and accelerate speed to performance make them a natural choice as training tools.

Competition and Globalization–In today's business world, it isn't enough to be the best company in your town, state, or country. Today, nearly every company in the world competes on a global playing field and faces increasing pressure and competition from companies located in other countries. With this increased competition, of course, comes the need to move faster and, as a result, increased pressure for good, quick, effective training that makes employees better than their competitors, no matter where the competitors may be located.

Technology–Perhaps the single most important factor contributing to the increased use, affordability, and availability of simulations is the advancement of technology.

Today, faster processors and new programming software continue to expand the horizons of computer-based simulations. Innovative simulation platforms like Regis Learning Solutions' SimPort™ simulation framework and SimWorks ™ simulation suite make it easier and more cost effective to build custom business simulations. Breakthroughs in adult learning, advances in video games, the internet, and the ability to cost-effectively develop and deliver rich multimedia all shape the future of simulations.

What will the future of business simulations hold? While the exact nature of potential advancements cannot be known, one thing is for certain: the possibilities are endless.

The Future of Simulations

Here are a few of the advancements that we predict will revolutionize business simulations–and workplace learning overall–in the years to come.

Head-to-head competition

Even the most advanced simulations today revolve around a single company. Within them, various teams assume leadership roles within a single organization and then compete against one another to see which team's version of the company outperforms the others.

But what about outside competition? In the real-world auto industry, competitors are many—an automotive company must consider Ford, GM, Volkswagon, and Toyota, among others. In this environment, market forces and competition—and how a company responds to these multiple outside variables—often dictate an organization's ultimate success or failure.

To their credit, today's simulations do incorporate these realities to an extent. Pre-programmed variables, for example, introduce learners to certain challenges. A primary competitor might slash its prices unexpectedly in an attempt to gain market share. Another might introduce a revolutionary new fuel-efficient vehicle to which consumers flock.

Within these current-generation simulations, however, such variables merely are a function of what simulation programmers or facilitators decide to program into the simulation; they are not necessarily an accurate reflection of what actually takes place, competitively, in the real world outside of the simulation.

The impending introduction of head-to-head competition promises to change all of that. Instead of simulations that incorporate only one company that all teams run separately, experiential learning solutions would incorporate head-to-head competition featuring many different companies from the same industry and allow teams of learners to compete against one another, just as competitors in the real world do.

Within such simulations, the impact of competitive market forces on companies would not be pre-programmed into the simulation. Rather, each team's actions would affect those of all other teams—creating a more free-flowing, organic, and responsive real-world microcosm of the competitive business environment.

Real-time, real-world input

Today's simulations, for the most part, incorporate fictional input. Learners progressing through a current-generation simulation might receive a fictional news alert informing them that a hurricane has destroyed the company's manufacturing facilities in a particular region of the world. Or a press release might introduce a competitor's latest product. These simulated events and communications mimic what *might* happen in the real world, yet they are not real.

The advent of real-time, real-world input, by contrast, would allow next-generation simulations to receive communications from the real world in real time—then seamlessly incorporate them into participants' learning experiences.

If CNN.com, for example, issues a morning report that an earthquake in Europe has destroyed several businesses, including several of the factories that the learners' simulated organization owns, this information would be input into the simulation automatically in real time, creating an incredibly lifelike microcosm of the real world and forcing learners to contend with the same challenges they would face on the job, yet in a safe environment.

Games and Entertainment

Games are not just for children, as we have seen, and they will quickly become an important part of corporate training. As the so-called Gen-X and younger generations spread across the workforce, games will force e-learning, simulations, and other computer training solutions to put on a "game face." The use of 3-D graphics and animated, life-like characters combined with engaging multi-dimensional storylines will expand the use and effectiveness of simulations. Participants will be pulled into a realistic environment that encourages exploration, competition, achievement, and team collaboration. Glimpses of the future can be found in video games like Blizzard's *World of Warcraft*, which allows players from all over the world to team up to create virtual armies and stage battles in graphically-rich, highly-competitive war games.

The promise of games in the workplace has already led organizations like the Woodrow Wilson Center for International Scholars in Washington, D.C. to create a consortium called the Serious Games Initiative. Their goal is to provide guidance in the creation of new games for policy education, exploration, and management. Games are already being used in the military, emergency services, city planning, and in healthcare—all showing promising results.

The entertainment value of games cannot be underestimated. In the next few years, game consoles will become the center of many living rooms as homes are equipped with direct links to high-definition television screens and DVDs. We're a society surrounded by rich media. Marshall McLuhan, famous for recognizing that the media would shape the western world, said that "anyone who tries to make a distinction between education and entertainment doesn't know the first thing about either."[29]

Intelligent Systems—Smart Models

Smart models with "minds of their own" will become essential to creating more realistic simulations. Models will not only be based on mathematical conditions, but they will evolve and change as they interact with the learners. In other words, the learners will not be the only ones learning. As individuals or teams run their simulated business, a competitive business run by the computer will respond with tactics of a formidable competitor. Learning from its mistakes and observing the actions of the human players, the computer will derive new ideas and attempt risky business decisions.

At any point in time, a snapshot of the model and human decisions can be captured and analyzed. From a learning perspective, employees can analyze various decisions and their impacts compared to the responses of the market and smart model. Essentially, the snapshots capture best and worse practices—your learners' intellectual capital.

Aside from offering educational and intellectual repository benefits, smart models will offer another benefit to organizations—the ability to play out "what if" scenarios at the time of need. Imagine that your organization has a new product and your research points to Europe as a high-growth market. Instead of depending on heroic effort and lots of money, the various what-if scenarios would be played out in a simulation. The simulation would give insight to potential investments in marketing and advertising, possible operational impacts on production and distribution, and of course, estimated returns on investments.

The Grid

Harnessing the power of grid computing to crunch snapshots of business simulations will provide insights far beyond what any other computer could offer. IBM's BIG BLUE at the Lawrence Livermore National Laboratory in California performs about 136 trillion computations a second. Grid computing at even 2-3 trillion computations a second will rapidly catch IBM's BIG BLUE computers at only a fraction of the price.

Advances in Haptics and virtual reality

Haptics, the science of touch, lets computer users interact with virtual worlds by feel. Video games are already taking advantage of Haptic devices, like the force-feedback steering wheels that torque and vibrate as a player navigates a virtual car down a bumpy road. Flight simulators are equipped with all kinds of Haptic devices that mimic the movements and resistance of flying a real plane. Surgeons use Haptics devices to practice their first incisions without actually cutting anyone.

Combine Haptic devices with virtual reality simulations, and employees will be able to work with millions of dollars' worth of equipment from their desktop computers. Virtually reality is the simulation of real or imagined environments that can be experienced visually in the three dimensions of width, height, and depth.

Employees would be able to practice fixing, disassembling, and assembling products from within a virtual reality simulation equipped with Haptic devices. Manufactures will be able to train their employees on machines in a safe simulated environment. The possibilities are limitless and will serve every aspect of training needs.

Business-to-business simulations

In the future, watch for business-to-business simulations that allow organizations from different but interdependent industries to train their employees together. While a tire manufacturer trains its employees on one simulation, for example, an automotive company might train its workers on a different, but connected, experiential learning solution.

This capability would allow the two simulations to interact with each other in such a way that the actions of one company would affect the other, just as they would in real life. Too many tires produced? Tire prices likely will fall and the auto manufacturer will benefit. Conversely, if there is a sudden car output shortage because there was a major earthquake that destroyed one of the auto manufacturer's plants, tires would have to be routed to another plant to be used.

The benefit of using business-to-business simulations would be that learners would not only have the opportunity to interact with other industries, just as they would while on the job, but also to better see and understand the complexities and challenges inherent to working within interdependent industries.

Mini-simulations

With the advent of smaller computer hardware and portable systems, "mini-simulations" could become available via handheld devices. Assessments would be deployed quickly in almost any environment, and the results quickly relayed to decision-makers. Learners would have access to simulation-based learning and analysis any time, anywhere. The possible reach of a mini-simulation is practically infinite.

Imagine, for example, taking a break from a high-stakes bargaining session and imputing new data into your cell phone, then instructing it to compute the most likely of outcomes, as well as what your best choices are for changing those outcomes if they are not what you want them to be.

Artificial life

The next big improvement for simulations will come in the form of artificial life (AL), also called software agents or intelligent agents. Simply put, AL is an independent program that would plug into a simulation environment–where it, in turn, would interact with other ALs and the learner and evolve according to those interactions. An AL controls its own actions, not its surrounding virtual environment. This means that for every situation, an infinite number of ALs could be plugged in to customize the learning for each user's individual needs.

It also should be noted that ALs are complex and possess human-like characteristics in terms of how they act and respond to certain scenarios; the computers develop preferences similar to a human's arbitrary likes and dislikes.

ALs also are capable of changing characteristics over time according to learners' interactions with them.

Imagine working at the customer-service desk of a real-world retail store. On the front line, you never know what type of person is going to approach you next; what her problem or issue, if any, will be; how she will handle the problem; how she will act toward you, and so forth. A training program with a virtual customer-service desk featuring many ALs would function in much the same way. ALs respond and adapt to events that occur in the virtual environment. For example, if a "hot-headed" AL walks up to the customer-service desk and the learner isn't polite, the AL might lose its temper. If the learner takes offense to this and starts yelling back, the two could quickly become involved in a screaming match. However, if the learner treats the same AL with as much courtesy as she can, the initial friction may not escalate. If the AL is reasonable, he eventually might calm down and listen to the learner. Then again, the AL might not be reasonable and might be looking for a fight -- no matter what.

Preparing to make a difficult sales call? A simulation AL could be harsher, more skeptical, and harder to convince than the real people the learner will try to convince while on the job, allowing you to practice your answers.

To further complicate a tutorial, several ALs might be placed in the same virtual environment. Suddenly, a simulated one-on-one business meeting becomes a conference. Not only do the ALs interact with the trainee, they interact with one another. This makes for the most realistic of learning environments, because the ALs create "relationships" with one another and with the learner. Two ALs might take a liking to each other, and one might back up what the other has to say at all times. Or one AL might be aggressive and attempt to run the meeting on her own, meaning that the learner and the other ALs constantly must struggle to keep the aggressive AL in check. Or perhaps one AL might be unprepared for the meeting and not as up to speed on the topic as the learner and the other ALs. Again, the training possibilities are as endless as the possible interactions in the real world.

The End of Training

The most important thing to remember as you continue to pursue a simulation as a training tool for your business in the years to come is that the simulation industry is changing and evolving rapidly. Technology, inevitably, will change. New advances will occur. And certain predictions made in this book -- and elsewhere, for that matter--will almost certainly prove inaccurate.

Yet, while this book will age and eventually grow dated, the basic principles that drive it will remain the same. Business simulations, no matter how they evolve, will successfully achieve their one primary purpose: Shorten the time it takes for employees to acquire new knowledge and skills to more effectively execute and evaluate business strategies.

---

[28] Lee, David B. "War Gaming: Thinking for the Future." *Air and Space Power Journal,* Summer 1990.

[29] McLuhan, Marshall." Thinkexist.com. 2005. <http://en.thinkexist.com/quotes/marshall_mcluhan/>

APPENDIX: SIMULATION TYPES

Common Simulation Types	Participant Role
Desktop (or Tabletop) Simulations are typically used in emergency response situations. Teams work together to quickly make decisions as a crisis continues to unfold. These simulations are best geared to training emergency response teams and executives.	*Active*
Role Simulations create an environment in which learners take on a role that evolves based on other simulation participants' reactions and responses to various situations. These simulations are best geared toward discovering a learner's strengths and weaknesses. They also can be used to introduce a learner to new ideas.	*Active*
Guided Simulations take a learner down a set of pre-determined paths. In such simulations, a leaner often is confronted with a few situations and is asked to select the best decision or course of action. Based on the learner's choice, the simulation then branches to another situation that builds upon the previous one. These types of simulations are best suited to making learners more familiar with new situations.	*Active*

Common Simulation Types	Participant Role
Goal-Directed Simulations are similar to guided simulations, but they also include a pre-defined goal that the learner tries to achieve. Games often fall into this category. Games provide motivation, structure, and a goal, thereby creating a supportive environment for learning. Goal-directed simulations are best suited for teaching specific skills and for more open-ended simulations, such as running a complex company where the goal is to make as much money as possible or to expand a company's operations into the global marketplace.	*Active*
Continuous Simulations continuously evolve as a result of changes over time. For example, the amount of fluid passing through a pipe may increase or decrease over time, but the flow is continuous. Therefore, the state of the simulation is determined at a specific point in time. Continuous simulations are most commonly used in situations like weather simulations, which model problems that have a constant flow in which the outputs are analyzed at specific time intervals.	*Observational*

Common Simulation Types	Participant Role
Discrete Simulations are usually used to model the effects that certain variables have on populations, systems, or sets of processes. In a discrete simulation, entities change state based on how a learner responds to various events. The passing of time does not have a direct effect, however. For example, orders arriving, products being developed, and products being shipped are examples of discrete events. Discrete simulations tend to provide more detail regarding the workings of a system than continuous simulation designs.	*Observational*
Responsive Simulations create an environment in which a learner takes on a role and is required to address many different situations and issues in parallel. Responsive simulations integrate role-based simulations with discrete and continuous simulations. They do not have any pre-determined paths. Rather, the simulation evolves or responds to the learner's thinking across many interconnected decisions. Responsive simulations tend to be the best solutions to real-world business issues, such as running a business, taking a product to market, and understanding the impacts that operations, sales, marketing, and finance have on one another. They also develop a learner's systems and critical-thinking skills.	*Active & Observational*

BIBLIOGRAPHY

Adkins, Sam S. "The 2002- 2010 U.S. Market for E-Learning Industry: The Shape of the Next Generation E-Learning Market." 2002. Brandon Hall.com. 15 July 2005 <http://www.brandon-hall.com/public/publications/market-sim/index.htm>.

Aldrich, Clark. *Learning By Doing: A Comprehensive Guide to Simulations, Computer Games, and Pedagogy in e-Learning and Other Education Experiences.* Hoboken, NJ: John Wiley & Sons, 2005.

Boehle, Sarah. "The Next Generation of E-Learning." *Training* Jan. 2005: 23 -31.

Collins, Jim. *Good to Great: Why Some Companies Make the Leap… and Others Don't.* New York: Harper Business, 2001.

Fritzsche, Dave, Nancy Leonard, Marian W. Boscia, and Phil Anderson. "Simulation Debriefing Procedures." *Developments in Business Simulation and Experiential Learning* 31 (2004): 337 - 338.

Gilbert, Thomas. *Human Competence: Engineering Worthy Performance.* New York: McGraw-Hill, 1978.

Greenleaf, Robert. "Motion and Emotion in Student Learning." *Education Digest* 69 (2003): 37- 42.

Hattie, John, and Richard Jaeger. "Assessment and Classroom learning: A deductive approach." *Assessment in Education: Principles, Policy & Practice* 5.1 (1998): 111- 23.

Hoffman, Thomas. "Simulations Revitalize E-Learning: E-learning Simulation Frameworks have Become Cheaper and Easier to Deploy." 2004. *Computer World.com.* 6 July 2005 <http://www.computer-world.com/careertopics/careers /training/story/0,10801,83639,00.html>.

Ilgen, Daniel, and Carol F. Moore. "Types and Choices of Performance Feedback." *Journal of Applied Psychology* 72 (1987): 401 - 06.

"Investment Banking: Increasing Demand for E-Learning Simulation." May 2004. *Katalyst.com.* 7 July 2005 <http://www.katalyst.com/IB/may2004Monitor.asp>.

Johnson, D.W., Skon, L., and Johnson, R. "Effects of Cooperative, Competitive, and Individualistic Conditions on Children's Problem-Solving Performance." *American Education Research Journal* 17 (1980): 83 - 93.

Larson, Carl, and Frank M.J. LaFasto. *Teamwork : What Must Go Right/What Can Go Wrong (SAGE Series in Interpersonal Communication).* Thousand Oaks, CA: SAGE Publications, 1989.

---. *When Teams Work Best: 6,000 Team Members and Leaders Tell What It Takes to Succeed.* Thousand Oaks, CA: SAGE Publications, 2001.

Mager, R. F., and Peter Pipe. *Analyzing Performance Problems or "You Really Oughta Wanna."* Atlanta: Center for Effective Performance, 1997.

Norton III, George M. *Valuation: Setting Sound Business Goals.* Indianapolis: Wiley Publishing, 2002.

Prensky, Marc. *Digital Game-Based Learning.* New York: McGraw-Hill, 2001.

Robinson, Dana Gaines, and James Robinson. *Performance Consulting: Moving Beyond Training*. San Francisco: Berrett-Koehler Publishers, 1996.

Skinner, Todd. *The Summit: Setting and Surpassing Extraordinary Business Goals*. Virginia Beach: Portfolio Publishing, 2003.

Smialek, Michael. "Driving Success through Performance Simulations." *Training Today* Mar./Apr. 2003: 3 - 5.

Summers, Gary J. "Today's Business Simulation Industry." *Simulation & Gaming* 35.2 (2004): 208–41.

"Training Managers' Forum: Onsite Customized Programs Reduce Per-capita Cost by 50%." Managing Training & Development Report Apr. 2005: 15.

"What Your Disaffected Workers Cost." *Gallup Management Journal.* 15 Mar. 2001. 15 July 2005 <http://gmj.gallup.com/content/default.asp?ci=439>.

Yager, Stuart, David W. Johnson, and Roger T. Johnson. "Oral Discussion, Group-to-Individual Transfer, and Achievement in Cooperative Learning Groups." *Journal of Educational Psychology* 77 (1985):60 - 66.